OPTIONS TRADING FOR BEGINNERS 2020

HOW TO TRADE FOR A LIVING WITH THE BASICS, BEST STRATEGIES AND ADVANCED TECHNIQUES ON DAY FOREX AND STOCK MARKET INVESTING (PASSIVE INCOME QUICK CRASH COURSE).

Table of Contents

Introduction 1

Chapter 1 What you need to know about Options Trading?. 4

Chapter 2 Tools and strategies for Option Trading............25

Chapter 3 Risk management and Market 67

Chapter 4 Variety of Options Trading 82

Chapter 5 Technical analysis 97

Chapter 6 Best Options Secret Strategies 126

Chapter 7 3 Actions for Intermediate Traders to Get Their Feet Wet..141

Chapter 8 Daily Routine for a Trader............................156

Conclusion 162

Introduction

Welcome and thank you very much for downloading options trading for beginners!

In this book, I'm going to introduce and demystify the world of options trading for you. Options trading sounds mysterious and complicated but the reality is it's pretty simple and you just need someone to explain it to you.

So, we're going to start this book by explaining the basics of what an option really is and how they are used to earn profits. Of course, all investing carries risk and that includes options trading. But one of the best things about options is they require relatively small amounts of capital to get started. So, you can experience some losses without causing any devastation. And if you're careful, you can avoid losses most of the time.

The key, of course, is understanding when to get in and out of trades and what strategies should be used to both minimize losses and increase the probability of profits.

I hope to cover this type of information for you in this book using plain English explanations so that you can get started trading as soon as possible. Now, I know from experience that not everyone who reads this book is going to follow my advice exactly, there are going to be some people that end up just losing money. That's just unfortunate because if you develop a solid trading plan with options, it's actually fairly easy to protect your investment account.

We will explain some of the big reasons that people end up losing money following this path.

Options trading isn't for everyone. It does require active involvement in the market, and you're going to have to follow the markets fairly closely in order to survive and make profits. So, let me state up front that if you are the kind of investor who just wants to set it and forget it, options probably aren't going to be of interest to you. They have a limited lifetime and they can gain or lose value very quickly and so it requires a lot of diligence and keeping up with what's going on with the markets to be successful. That said, options aren't nearly as complicated as people imagine. So if you're a little bit leery about becoming actively involved in your trading, let me suggest that you give it a chance and read the book before deciding whether or not options trading is something that you can include as part of your investment plans.

Finally, a word about investing and trading in general. If you are brand-new to options, one thing that you need to understand is that options trading is done for the purpose of making profits over the short term. So, we are talking about her in cash over a 2 to 3-week period, generally speaking. Options trading is not about long-term investing or even something like swing trading over the course of months. Although, there are some options that last out to two years and we will talk a little bit about those as well.

Chapter 1 What you need to know about Options Trading?

What An Option Is?

An option is a contract that gives an individual the right to purchase or sell an underlying instrument at a strike price before or on a particular date. One breaks down options into call option or a put option. A call option gives the buyer the right to buy an underlying asset at a predetermined price within a specified time. A put option gives the buyer the right to sell underlying security during a particular time and at a preset price. It is important to note that while options contract provides the buyer the right to purchase or sell, it does not give them any obligations to trade.

One also classifies options as derivatives. A derivative is a financial instrument with monetary value that comes from an underlying asset. It is an agreement between two or more parties, and it obtains its price or worth from variations of the underlying benchmark or asset. An option is, therefore, a derivative of financial securities because its price depends on the cost of another asset. Options are a class of assets that can offer someone several advantages in trading when they apply them correctly.

Options Basics

In this chapter, we are going to talk more about the details of options. We are also going to learn all of the jargon that is associated with the options markets and learn how to find options to trade.

Call Option

We have already discussed a little bit about what call options are. But let's give a more formal definition. If you opt to purchase a call option, you are essentially purchasing the opportunity to buy 100 shares of the stock at a fixed price.. So, all you need to do is remember that a call option is a specific opportunity for you to purchase 100 shares of stock. Also, the value of call options goes up as share price rises.

Put Option

This option is the opposite of the call option, in that it seeks to profit from a decline in share price. The buyer of a put option has the right to sell 100 shares of stock at the strike price. If the price of shares drops below the strike price, the buyer is at a distinct advantage. They can buy shares on the option market and then sell them at the higher strike price. The value of put options increases if share price declines.

Exercising an Option

If the buyer of an option exercises their right to buy the shares, we say that they are exercising their right. The seller of the option is then "assigned", that is they are under assignment to sell the shares.

For a put option we say the buyer of the option is exercising their right if they sell the shares to the originator of the contract. Once again, the seller of the option would be assigned.

There are two styles of options. An American style option is one that can be exercised on or before the expiration date of the option. A European style option is one that can only be exercised on the expiration date.

The Main Reason People Write Options Contracts

You can enter into an options contract by logging into your brokerage and selling the options contract to open your position. The reason that you would do this is that you can sell an options contract for a fee which is called the premium. When you sell an options contract to enter a position, you get to keep the premium as profit no matter what happens. In a nutshell, this is the reason why people sell options contracts - to generate monthly income.

There are some risks involved in doing so. If you sell a call contract, the risk is that you are going to have to sell the underlying shares. So, for example, if you own 100 shares of IBM and open a call contract on those shares, the risk is that you will have to sell the shares.

Someone who was using this strategy would probably be hoping that they could profit by selling the options contract to use as a source of monthly income, while keeping the shares. A common strategy is doing it right to be able to sell another options contract the following month. This way you would be able to make some more income from the premium. That works most of the time, but sometimes it is not going to work. If the share price rises above the strike price you selected, you could be assigned and have to sell the shares.

People sell put options for the same reason – to earn monthly income. When you sell a put contract, the risk is that you will have to buy the stock and do so at a high price. So, if someone exercises the contract, you better have access to cash in order to purchase the 100 shares of stock behind the contract.

In most circumstances, the option is never going to be exercised, which is what people are counting on when making put contracts. This way, they basically earn money by selling the put option contract which really is based on nothing. Actually, that is not entirely true. A seller of a put contract is making money on the risk that they are taking by setting up the contract. That is, they assume the risk from someone else. It could be interpreted as someone buying "insurance" on their stock.

Of course, depending on the amount of cash that you need to come up with to purchase stock, the risk could be significant. The real risk is determined by how much the stock has dropped. So at least there is a lower limit to it.

Options Chains (or tables)

These are just lists of options that can be bought or sold. They are grouped by date and then sorted by price. Call and put options are separated or displayed side by side.

Strike Price

One of the most important characteristics of an options contract is called the strike price. The strike price is simply the price the shares of stock would be bought or sold for if the option contract was actually exercised. The relationship between the price of the shares on the market and the strike price will determine, in part, the price of the option if it is traded. The strike value is one of the most critical things that you need to look at. When you open up options tables you are going to find that they are listed in order by the strike price for each date. We already saw that when we looked at AMD prices for options on Robin Hood.

When we look at the options for Apple, we see that they are listed in terms of strike price on the left-hand side. You cannot see that below in this screenshot (it is black because it's after hours). The share price is shown at the center of the screen, which is $194.22. The prices on the left-hand side, which denote that the options are calls, are the strike prices.

The price in the box or inside the button on the right-hand side is the price of the actual options contract. You can see that some other information is provided, such as how much the price went up or down today (these look pretty good for Apple, you can see that some gained 30% or more), as well as the percent change needed to get to break even. Break-even is the price that the option must attain in order for you to have no net profit or loss. This will be the strike price plus the price paid for the option for a call, or the strike price minus the price paid for the option for a put.

The strike price of an option never changes. It is set when the options contract is written or sold for the first time. So, if you see an option for Apple that has a strike price of a $193, that strike price remains the same until the option expires, in which case the option no longer exists. So, remember that it is just a fixed quantity, which is a permanent feature of the options contract. Also remember that the strike price and its relationship with the market price is going to be the central factor in determining whether or not the option can be sold at a profit.

Calls and Puts

With basic options, you can perform two types of operations on underlying security (that is, the financial instrument). One type of contract allows you to buy the security for a certain price, and the other will enable you to sell it. Do note that you are not under any obligation to buy or sell and that you can allow the contract to expire without taking any action.

The call option contract is what allows you to buy the security and the put allows you to sell it. Every option's purchase, being a contract, comes with stipulations and associated terminology.

Learn the Lingo

The first piece of terminology you have to grapple with is the concept of the premium. Despite the fancy name, the premium is simply the name given to the price of the contract. So why not call it the price? Well, this is because of the way the price arrives. Black-Scholes complexity aside, every option contract's premium has two components to it: the intrinsic value and the time value.

There is a third volatility value as well but let's ignore that for now. The intrinsic value is simply the difference between the price at which the option becomes valuable and the current price of the security. The time value is a price associated with how much time is left on the contract.

So at what price does the option become valuable? Well, this is called the strike price. The strike price is the threshold beyond which you can exercise the option. So if you buy a call (the right to buy) with a strike price of $10 and the current market price of the underlying is $5, your option has no intrinsic value since the strike price is above the market price.

Every contract has an expiration date with the most heavily traded ones being the ones expiring within a month. The time left for the option to expire is the key factor in determining how much time value the option has. If your call still has two months to expire, then there is a greater possibility of the market price exceeding the strike price, than if the option were expiring tomorrow.

Therefore, the former option would have a higher time value than the latter. Generally speaking, the closer you get to the expiration date, the lesser the time value is. The third factor in pricing is the volatility value. Briefly, the more volatile the underlying is, the greater this value.

Volatility refers to how far and how fast security moves. Volatile securities usually move very quickly and are thought of as being unpredictable thanks to their quick movements. Given this unpredictability, it is natural that the person selling you the option should be compensated for the risk they're undertaking.

The relation of the market price to the strike price has further terminology associated with it. In the case of a call, when the strike price is above the market price, the option is said to be "out of the money." When they're equal, it is said to be "on/at the money." When the strike price is lesser than the market price, the option is "in the money."

The reasoning behind this terminology is this. A call is valuable only when the market price increases beyond the strike price. Think about it. You're buying the option to give you the right to purchase the underlying. If the current market price is $5, the only calls that will make you a profit are those with strike prices below $5.

In anticipation of a rising market, traders often buy higher strike price options. So, if a trader buys a $10 strike price call, they're anticipating that the market will increase beyond this price before the option expires.

Using this logic, can you figure out how the terminology works for a put? When is a put in the money?

Well, a put gives you the right to sell the underlying. So the only valuable puts will be the ones with a strike price higher than the current market price. Hence, with puts, when the strike price is greater than the market price, a put is said to be in the money. When the put's strike price is lower than the market price, it is out of the money. In other words, it is directly opposite to the call's conditions.

So what happens when you buy an option? Well, you pay the premium and then wait to see if you want to exercise it or not or sell if for a higher premium to someone else. You could also let it expire without doing anything. In all cases, the maximum size of your loss is limited to the premium you paid to buy the option.

I want to point out that irrespective of your trade moving into the money or not, you will forfeit the option premium. So when you enter an option trade, you're placing yourself at a loss right from the start. The good news is that this is your maximum loss. In a stock trade, your potential loss is the difference between the market price and zero, since every stock can turn worthless.

For example, if you buy AMZN at $246, your potential loss is -$246 per share. However, if you buy a call option, your maximum loss is the price of the option. If AMZN doesn't make it past the call's strike price, it doesn't matter for you since you don't own the stock and you don't have any obligation to buy it.

When you short a stock, that is, sell first before seeking to buy it back at a lower price, your potential loss is unlimited. This is because a stock can rise to infinite levels without stopping. If you shorted AMZN at $246, your potential loss is unlimited per share. It could rise to $1000, or $2000 and so on. Your maximum gain is $246 per share since it can only fall till zero.

However, if you buy a put option on AMZN, your maximum loss is capped at the option's premium while your maximum gain is capped at your option's price plus $246 since this is the maximum amount by which it could fall. The $246 will be added to the intrinsic value portion of the premium.

Here we see the major benefit of options which is their ability to cap your maximum risk. With stock trading, you can do this via a stop-loss order, but markets are notorious for jumping stop-loss levels due to liquidity concerns. Liquidity is a fundamental concept you need to understand to trade successfully.

Many traders, while first starting think that every price in the market will be honored and that transactions can occur at every level. This is not the case. Think of it as going to an actual market of say, fruits. If you want to sell your apples for $10, you will find a certain number of takers. If you want to sell it for $10,000, unless God blessed those apples personally, you're not going to find any takers.

There's no liquidity for apples at the $10,000 price. The same thing happens in the stock market all the time. When a stock moves violently, it often skips multiple levels, and it is quite common for an illiquid stock to skip right past the stop loss level. The broker can only execute your orders at the prevailing market price, so if that price happens to be multiple points lower than your stop loss, you have to eat the loss.

Options don't have any such dangers attached to them. Your maximum loss is fixed right at the start, and that's it.

Exercising and Quotes

The expiration date refers to the time when the option contract will expire. Beyond this time, you cannot exercise your option. Now, whether you can apply it before this time depends on the type of option you have purchased. There are two types of options when it comes to exercisability: American and European.

European options can be exercised only on the expiration date. This makes them a great option for institutional hedging purposes since the date is fixed, and the pricing model that applies to them is a lot easier. As such, European options don't provide much potential for speculation.

American options, on the other hand, can be exercised at any point prior to the expiry date. This makes them great for speculation. Interestingly, American options are difficult to price correctly due to the varying exercisability dates. The Black Scholes model is designed for pricing European options. The price extends to American ones because it is close enough under conditions of steady volatility.

However, when an instrument begins to behave outside of its historical parameters, Black Scholes is incapable of pricing anything. This is why it is possible to find great bargains in the options markets. None of the strategies in this book are dedicated to finding Black Scholes mispricings, but you can explore these if you're interested.

Either way, thanks to their nature, I'll be focusing exclusively on American options in this book. Next, you need to understand how options quotes work. The option chain is at the heart of every broker's display with regards to trading options. The chain is called as such because it usually lists a range of strike prices for a given expiration date.

The filters for an option chain interface is as follows: The type of option (call or put) and the expiration date of the contract. Options which expire in the current month are called current or front month options. Ones expiring next month are called a far month. The expiration dates for contracts beyond the far month depend on which expiration cycle has been assigned to the stock. Due to a large number of stocks being traded, every stock is randomly assigned one of three cycles. The three cycles run as:

January, April, July, October

February, May, August, November

March, June, September, December.

So if you want to buy an option on a stock which is assigned to the first chain in August, you'll see options expiring in August (front month), September (far month), October, January, and April. This way, there are always options available for three months at a time for traders to speculate in.

There are longer-term options with expiration dates over a year away. These are called LEAPS. LEAPS are less liquid, and you should be careful speculating in these. If you want to take advantage of a fundamental fact or a Black Scholes mispricing, LEAPS are ideal. For now, understand that the best speculative opportunities reside in the current and near month options.

Cashing out your options

A position refers to your holdings in the market. If you've bought a call on AMZN, this is a position. There are different positions you can adopt in the market when trading options. Generally speaking, there are two types of positions when it comes to trading any instrument: a long and a short.

A long refers to you buying the instrument in anticipation of its price rising, and a short refers to you selling the instrument in anticipation of its price falling. Options are no different, but the implications of shorting options are different than with stocks. First, the language is a bit different when referring to shorting an option. A person who shorts an option is called the writer. The buyer is called a buyer, so there's no change there.

Here are the different types of positions you can hold with options:

Long call- This is when you're buying a call in anticipation of the price rising.

Long put- This is when you buy a put in anticipation of the price falling. All good so far.

Short call- Here, you're writing a call with the anticipation that the price of the underlying will not rise beyond the strike price. Some strategies use it for purposes other than this, but generally, this is the intention. Note that you're not explicitly betting on the price falling, like with a put, bit simply that the price does not rise beyond a certain point. This is an important distinction.

Short put- This is when you write a put betting on the fact that price will not fall beyond a certain level. Same as with the above scenario, its intention is different from that of a long call.

Writing options is a tricky business and calls for extremely good risk management. Generally, your broker will not allow you to write options unless safeguards are in place. The short call is the riskiest position you can adopt in the market unless it happens to be covered.

If you think about the mechanics of how this trade would work, you'll see why this is. Let's say the market price of the underlying is $5. You short the $10 near month call betting that by the end of next month, the price is going to remain below $5. When you write an option, you receive the premium the buyer pays, and this is your maximum profit.

Essentially, the maximum loss that the buyer can experience is your maximum profit. If the price does go beyond $10, your loss is unlimited. You'll have to buy the underlying at whatever price it is in the market and sell it for $10 to the call buyer. If the price rises to $50, your loss is $40 per share. What if it rises to $1000? You'll likely go bankrupt because a single contract covers 100 shares.

While the maximum loss is not unlimited with the short put, similar risks exist. Therefore, your broker will require you to own the stock or have some other arrangement which covers the huge risk. For example, you can write a call if you own the underlying stock. This way, you don't need to go out and buy the stock or claim bankruptcy in case the option moves into the money.

My point is that when it comes to option writing, you need to manage your risk very carefully and always ensure that your position is covered. The strategies in this book require you to write options, but all of them will be covered, so the risk is always capped at an acceptable level.

More Lingo

Options are most commonly available for stocks and FX pairs. If you're a resident or citizen of the US, then it is highly unlikely that you can trade FX options. Therefore you're limited to stocks. However, this is like saying you're limited to all of America, and that is a pretty big place indeed.

When you trade stock options, there are some other terms you'll run into. Let's take a look at these briefly:

Open interest- Open interest refers to the total number of contracts that are available for a given strike price. OI often gives important clues especially before important announcements since it indicates which direction the market could move in. For our purposes, this isn't very relevant.

Implied Vol- Implied vol stands for implied volatility and is a historical measure of the stock's volatility. This is an important component of the Black Scholes formula and is used to calculate the price of the option.

Delta- This is a member of what is called the 'Greeks' within options trading. The Greeks are a bunch of Greek letters, each of which symbolizes a different measurement of the option's volatility and behavior. The delta is the rate at which the price of the option changes with every unit change in the price of the underlying. For obvious reasons, options with a high delta are desirable although they are likely to go pear-shaped sooner as well.

There are a few other terms that can be explored. However, I won't list them here since they're used almost exclusively by institutional traders and it is unlikely any of these terms will affect your trading.

This brings to a close our look at options basics. The last bit of terminology we saw is not essential to understand the strategies we'll talk about later, but you should know them since they'll be floating around on your screen. Speaking of screens, this will be provided by your broker, and the quality of your broker will determine your profitability.

So let's get to know them better!

Chapter 2 Tools and strategies for Option Trading

One of the most complex issues in options trading is options trading strategies, especially because many traders are not familiar with it. There are very many strategies that can be employed when trading options and each has its unique characteristic. Each has a unique set of options spread and may involve strategies like combining different positions into one overall position based on the underlying security.

While some strategies are simple and straightforward, others are complex and involve many components. Although you do not have to have a working knowledge of each of them, you will more likely achieve success and make consistent money when trading options if you know all the good ones and when to use them.

The best Options Trading platforms and software's

Right before we jump into the strategies, you need to know how to pick a good one. Adopting the appropriate strategy in every instance is difficult because there are many to choose from, and each scenario comes with its unique factors. In addition, the choice you make will determine how successful you will be. Therefore, you need to learn this skill.

It is okay to buy options and sell them later near or on the expiry date. This could still earn you a profit, but a modest one. Some investors choose to conduct their business this way. However, to get the real money, you need to employ a number of strategies and ensure that you use the right options spread for each scenario.

Succeeding in options trading does not just require an accurate forecast of where underlying security is headed, the trading the related options. You should aim at maximizing your returns taking into consideration the amount you have invested and the measure of risk exposure. Use the following factors to pick out the right trading strategy:

1. Determine your outlook: the outlook is the direction you expect the price to head to, either fall or rise. There are four potential outlooks. The bearish expects the price to fall, and the bullish expects a price rise, the neutral expects the price to be relatively stable while the volatile expects some significant price changes. Although this adds to the number of considerations you make, it also

means that you will have more opportunities to make money.

2. Weigh out the risks versus the rewards: Different strategies have different risk profiles. Some have limited while others have fixed maximum losses. Measuring them out with the help of a risk/reward ratio will help you weigh out what you stand to gain versus what you could lose.

3. Options spread versus a single position: Options trading strategies often require creating spreads by combining different positions to an overall position. This reduces risks significantly, reduces the costs of taking a position or creates merely a position from which that can accommodate more than one outcome. This makes a spread better than a single position. However, the commissions paid for a single position is less. In addition, the trader stands to receive higher returns unlike when using the spreads, which limit profitability.

4. Your trading level: The trade level assigned by your broker could influence the trading strategy you pick up. Trading levels are assigned to prevent customers from taking higher risks than necessary. Therefore, a low trading level will limit strategies that increase the risk

level, allowing them to be used only in higher trading levels.

5. The strategy's complexity: The strategies themselves come with their own degrees of complexity. Some are relatively simple and only require one or two transactions while others are complex and will require three or more transactions. This makes it essential to consider this fact one of the reasons being that the more transactions you will need to perform, the higher the brokerage fees you pay. High fees significantly affect the returns, especially when your investment is small. Many transactions also make it harder to determine the potential profits and losses of a trade and to identify the most appropriate price movements. Discovering the right entry and exit points of a position also becomes difficult with complex transactions, while it is one of the most critical aspects of planning a trade. This does not mean that you should keep off all complex strategies, it only means that you should make careful considerations before picking any of them.

After the head scratcher that is the Iron Condor, we've now come to a far simpler bunch of strategies to understand. Credit spreads involve both puts and calls and also can be classified as vertical or horizontal. A good way to look at them is to in fact look at them in this manner.

They can be used in both bullish and bearish conditions and also lend themselves very well to different volatility conditions.

Vertical Spreads

Vertical spreads are so named because of the way they occur in the options chain. Vertical spread trades usually involve just calls or just puts and involve buying or selling a higher strike price against buying or selling a lower strike price. Thus, a spread is formed and since the strike prices are listed vertically, this creates a vertical looking spread.

Despite the word credit in the name, these strategies can be net debit or net credit strategies on entry. Remember this refers to whether you pay money out of pocket to enter or whether you get paid to enter. Net credit trades tend to realize their maximum profits upon entry while net debits have higher ceilings and realize the maximum loss upon entry.

Which strategy you choose to deploy depends on the existing volatility conditions and this should inform whether a put or a call spread will work better for you. Anyway, let's first begin by looking at bull call spreads.

Bull Call Spread

The bull call spread has two legs within it:

An at the money long call

An OTM short call

As you can see, this is a far easier trade to establish compared to what we've just looked at with the Iron Condor. The idea is to profit in an uptrending market that is moving upwards slowly. This will work in market conditions such as ones towards the end of a trend where the participation in the market from both sides (buy and sell) is high and the trend will soon be moving into a massive range.

This tends to be the default state of the market for the most part so it is a very profitable strategy you can employ. Furthermore, you don't need to understand or even take into account the Greeks when adopting this strategy.

First, you buy a near month call which is close to the money or at the money. Next, you write a higher strike price call which is out of the money. The idea is that you'll earn the premium from the stock's upward movement. Your maximum profit will be capped at the strike price at which you wrote the call.

This strike price will determine your maximum profit as a percentage of your account. Remember, the structure of this trade means that it is a net debit trade. Let's see how the math works out.

Using GOOG as an example again, we see that the current trading price is 1229. The closest near month at the money call would be the one at 1230 which cost 33.50 to buy. Next, we need to figure out which strike price to sell. Let's say we choose the 1260 strike which nets us 19.50 as a credit. Our cost of entry works out as:

Cost of entry = cost of long call - premium earned from short call = 33.5-19.5 = $14 per share.

Maximum gain = strike price of sort call - strike price of long call - cost of entry = 1260-1229-14 = $17 per share.

So how much does $17 per share work out to in terms of a profit percentage for your account? Well, this depends on the size of your capital. Either way, use this calculation to figure out how much of a maximum loss you will need to stomach in order to earn the maximum gain.

These strike price levels will be your primary exit points. So what happens if you need to adjust it? Well, adjusting a spread trade is quite easy. You simply roll it up or down as you would a collar. Of course, before adjusting the trade you will need to figure out whether your primary assumptions are still valid.

If they are, go ahead and adjust the trade as needed. Keep your risk numbers in mind by figuring out your maximum loss.

Bear Call Spread

Let's say you encounter a sideways market or a mildly bearish one. You dont think Iron Condors are your cup of tea as yet so want something that's easier to implement and understand. This is where the bear call spread comes in. Like the bull call spread this trade has two legs to it:

A short at or slightly out of the money call

A long OTM call

The primary instrument in this strategy is the short call which is as close to the current market price as possible. As the market price falls or remains within a tight range, the premium of the short will keep decreasing. In order to cover the call you wrote, you will need a long call and this is where buying the OTM call comes into play.

The premium from the ATM call will be higher than the premium you will pay for the OTM call and hence, this is a net credit trade. The maximum amount you will earn from this trade is realized upfront in other words. Take care that the volatility is decreasing when you enter this trade.

Increasing volatility means you will need to move further out of the money and this will decrease your maximum gain thanks to the premiums decreasing. Set your primary and secondary exit points well in advance. Determining your primary exit point is done in the same way as with the bull call spread.

Let's work through an example to see how it plays out. Using GOOG's market price of 1229, we can write the 1230 call which will net us 33.50 in premium per share. We'll buy the 1260 call which costs us 24.40.

Thus our maximum gain or net credit on entry is:

Maximum gain = Premium earned from short call - premium paid for long call = 33.5-24.4 = $9.10 per share.

Maximum loss = strike price of long call - strike price of short call + premium earned on entry = 1260-1230-9.1 = $20.9 per share

As you can see, the risk reward of this strategy is skewed with us risking more than what we earn. First, as mentioned previously, this is an example so the conditions necessary for an ideal bear call spread might not be present in GOOG. Having said this, net credit trades always have skewed reward to risk ratios.

So what is the advantage of using them? Won't this mean we'll consistently lose money in the long term since the loss amounts are higher than the max gain? Well, not quite. While the reward to risk ratio might be skewed, the odds of the trade working out depend on the volatility.

This is why it's very important to note the volatility of the stock before you enter. Also, the presence of s/r levels is crucial. In this strategy, you don't want price to move beyond a certain level, which is the strike price of the short call. Thus, placing it beyond a strong resistance level is ideal. You don't need to hold this trade till expiry. Simply take advantage of the time decay and close your trade before expiry if you feel like it.

Adjustment is pretty straightforward, as it is with all spread trades. You simply roll the spread upwards or down depending on your analysis.

Bull Put Spread

You can create spreads even in puts and the bull put spread aims to take advantage of the same type of market conditions that the bull call spread does. In rising markets, especially those with rising volatility, the bull put spread will help cover your downside and give you a huge upside.

The trade consists of two legs like with all spread trades:

A short ATM put

A long OTM put

The primary money making instrument in this trade is the short put. The key is to get as close to the market price as possible. Another way of increasing your overall profit on the trade is to have the OTM put as close as possible to the ATM put. This reduces your margin of error but it will increase your reward.

Establish the long leg of the trade prior to the short in order to avoid any drama from your broker. The long leg covers the short, hence the order. Due to the fact that there's nothing capping the upside movement of the stock, this strategy is far more suitable and accommodates higher levels of volatility, unlike the bull call spread which has a hard cap. While the gain you would make here is also limited, it does result in an average gain that is higher than the bull call spread. Let's look at an example.

GOOG's market price is 1229 so our first task is to establish the long portion of this trade. Assuming the presence of a significant support just above it, let's choose the 1190 strike as appropriate for our long position. This will cost us 21.80 to enter. For our short leg, we want to get as close to the money as possible and 1220 seems like a good choice.

Now, you can go closer but remember you don't want the trade to go against you if it experiences a very small movement. Hence, pick an appropriate level on the basis of s/r levels. Either way, writing the 1220 put nets us 27.50 as a credit. Hence, our maximum gain in this trade is:

Maximum gain = premium earned from short put - premium paid for long put = 27.50- 21.8 = 5.70 per share.

Our maximum loss is the difference between the strike prices subtracted by our net credit:

Maximum loss = Strike price of short put - strike price of long put - net credit = 1220-1190-5.7 = 24.30 per share.

Again we see that a net credit strategy results in a skewed reward to risk ratio. This is a normal thing, as discussed in the previous section, and your technical analysis should back up your selection of strike prices.

Adjusting the trade is pretty straightforward. You simply roll it up or down depending on what your analysis tells you. If you find that your initial analysis was invalid, exit the trade and go back to the drawing board.

You might be wondering when you ought to choose a bull call spread versus a bull put spread? After all, both of them seek to take advantage of the same market environments, for the most part. However, the volatility should guide your decision and I'll discuss this in the section later on in this chapter regarding adjustments.

Bear Put Spread

The bear put spread aims to take advantage of a downtrending market. Like the bull call spread, it is a net credit trade and has two legs as a part of it:

A short OTM put

A long ATM put

The primary profit instrument in this trade is the long put which will increase in price as the underlying price decreases. The short put reduces the price of the long put and also caps the maximum loss you will incur as part of this trade.

Again, here we see that you can choose your maximum loss according to whatever size your account is. This makes risk management very straightforward and this is a quality of all spread trades. With more sophisticated strategies like the Iron Condor, you need to constantly be evaluating what your risk is and in many cases, rolling your trade will result in doubling your risk.

There is no such risk in the vertical spread trades, or even horizontal for that matter as we'll soon see. For now, let's look at how the trade works using GOOG as an example with its market price at 1229.

Let's assume that conditions are bearish and GOOG has just hit a significant resistance it is going to take some time to get past. As always, pick the near month puts in order to fully capture the time decay inherent within them. So for our first leg, which is the long put, let's choose 1220 as our strike price and this is going to cost us $33 in premium.

Next, we establish the short leg which needs to be out of the money so let's pick 1200 as our strike price. This is going to yield us 22.20 in premium. So the math works out as such:

Cost of entry = cost of long premium - cost of short premium = 33-22.2 = 10.80 per share.

Maximum gain = strike price of long put - strike price of short put = 1220-1200 = 20 per share.

Your strike prices will be your primary exit points. In case you wish to adjust your trade, you need to earmark secondary exit points beforehand. You can adjust your trade by either choosing to roll it to the secondary points or change its structure altogether. Before we get into the ins and outs of adjustment, let's look at horizontal spreads.

Horizontal Spreads

Horizontal spreads are also called calendar spreads. This is because they are time neutral in that unlike with vertical spreads, the expiry dates of both legs of the trade exist in different months. This creates a horizontal structure in terms of the way it is depicted in the option chain.

Horizontal spreads can be used to take advantage of both bullish and bearish conditions as you'll see.

Call Calendar Spread

The call calendar spread is a bullish horizontal spread and has two legs as a part of it.

Long term long call

Short term short call

The idea behind this spread is to take advantage of when a stock is experiencing sluggish movement. Let's say you identified GOOG as headed into strong resistance at 1230, which is where the market price is close to at the moment. You thus know that in the short term, it is unlikely to move past this level but in the long term it looks pretty likely to move upwards.

Both calls have the same strike price which needs to be as close to the money as possible. The only difference is that the short term call expires within the month or the near month and the long term call expires at least a month after the short term call. Let's look at GOOG and see how this would play out at this point in time.

The closest ATM strike price is the 1230 level and this is going to earn us 33.5 per share upon writing it. The same level is selling for 48.50 per share in the far month which is two months away from the current date.

Cost of entry = cost of long call - premium received from short call = 48.5-33.5 = 15 per share.

The reward calculation is not as straightforward as with other spreads. For one thing we need the short term call to expire worthless. After that, whatever rise takes place in the stock will be reflected in the option premium of the long call and hence will be captured when we exit the trade.

Put Calendar Spread

The put calendar spread is executed less often that the call calendar spread. Why this happens is not known really. Generally speaking, people are less inclined to take the short side of the market than they are the long so perhaps this has something to do with it.

The premise of the put calendar spread is the same as the call calendar except this applies to bearish conditions. A stock looks like it has hit support and might stay there for some time before moving downwards. So we short the nearer option and go long on the longer term put with the same strike price.

Like the call spread, it is a net debit trade which means you need to pay in order to enter the trade. Given that the math works in the exact same way as the call calendar spread, I'm not going to bore you again with it. By this point, you've hopefully internalized it anyway.

The profit calculation also works in the same manner with us expecting or needing the short term put to expire worthless. You can exit before this of course but that comes under the heading of adjustment and there are a few things you need to consider before doing that.

Adjustments

So now you've learned all about vertical and horizontal spreads and which sort of market conditions they work in. There are two major things that need to be addressed here. First, should you change a vertical spread into a horizontal spread and if yes, when should you do this? Second, the vertical spread strategies take advantage of similar market conditions. So which ones should you choose?

Let's tackle the first question. Should you be changing vertical spreads to horizontal or vice versa? Well, if you're changing a horizontal spread to a vertical one, you need to have some very good reasons to do so. This is because the horizontal spread is more of a cruise control trade. If you happen to see a volatility spike that is going to lead to quicker price action, then by all means go ahead and change it. Depending on which spread you have on, you'll be faced with the choice of a vertical call or put spread.

Changing a vertical spread to a horizontal one works in reverse. If volatility decreases to the extent that the stock simply stops moving, although this is very rare, or if your spreads are just too far away, consider changing it to a horizontal spread. It won't rescue your trade in any way but it might make you more money.

To be frank, most changes like this happen when the trader has misread the market and now wants to mitigate this. There's nothing wrong with this approach, I'm just stating it as a fact. So always examine your assumptions and really work on your technical and s/r skills.

Now, onto the second question. In a bullish environment, should you choose a bull call spread or a bull put? In a bearish environment, should you go with a bear call or bear put? In order to figure this out, we need to look at our old friend volatility again. This bit is nowhere near as complicated as that.

The figure you want to be looking at is the implied volatility. When this figure is low, historically speaking, options will be fairly priced and will favor buyers of options (Beaty, 2019). Conversely, when implied vol is high, you should be a seller since options will have a significant volatility premium built into them. As volatility decreases, you can capture this decay along with the time decay for a double charge to your profits.

Hence, when implied vol is high, stick with the strategies that require you to be a buyer of options that is the bull call spread (in case of bullishness) and bear put spread (in case of bearishness). When implied volatility is low, stick to the bull put or bear call spreads.

Another way of looking at this, and simplifying this for you, is to go for a net debit trade when implied vol is low and net credit trade when implied vol is high.

This brings to a close our look at credit (and debit) spread trades. As you can see, there's a lot going on here but it isn't anywhere near as complicated as the Iron Condor. Again, you don't need complexity to master the markets. Simply focus on what you can execute the best and you will see success.

Next, we're going to look at another slightly complex strategy, the double diagonal. Don't worry though, this is an extremely creative strategy which you can deploy in all sorts of markets and when mastered, will give you another excellent tool for your options trading toolkit.

Strategies for new Options traders

Below is a comprehensive description of some of the best and commonly used strategies with accompanying advice on how to use them in different scenarios.

The Long Call Strategy

This strategy is ideal for investors who are aggressive and quite bullish about a stock. It is, however, the most basic of the trading strategies and is relatively easy to understand. Buying calls could be an excellent way of capturing the potential of this strategy with the least amount of risk, and when you buy, you expect the price on a stock to rise.

You can use this strategy when dealing with one or two call options

The ideal time to employ this strategy is when you feel very bullish about the stock

The risk involved can only affect the premium, it can only happen if the market expires or the option strike price falls to zero.

The rewards of taking up this strategy are unlimited

Its breakeven price is the sum of the premium and the strike price.

The Basic Margin, including the self-directed investment accounts, are eligible

The Long Put Strategy

This strategy differs from the Long Call. To understand this one, you must remember that the opposite of buying a call is purchasing a put. This strategy is ideal for when the investor is feeling bearish and buys a put option. A put option will give him the right to sell his stock to a Put seller at a preset price, limiting his risk. This makes the long put an ideal strategy to use to take advantage of a falling market.

The best time to take up a long put strategy is when the investor is feeling bearish about the direction of the stock price

It presents a limited risk to the premium amount

The rewards are limited

The breakeven price is the strike price subtract the premium (Strike Price − Premium)

The Short Call Strategy

The strategy of a long call differs from the strategy of a short call. The long call is used when you expect the stock prices to rise, but if you expect the prices of the underlying stock to fall, you take up the short call strategy. An investor takes up this strategy when feeling very bearish about the stock prices.

This position offers limited potential for returns, and an investor could likely incur large losses if the underlying price begins to increase rather than decrease. Although this strategy is easily executed, it can be risky especially because of the unlimited risk the seller of a call is exposed to.

In summary:

This strategy is best used when the investor is very bearish about a stock

It offers unlimited risk

The profits or rewards are limited to the premium

The breakeven price is the sum of the premium and the strike price

The Short Put Strategy

We say that when an investor is bearish about the stock price, he uses along Put strategy. However, selling a Put option is the opposite of buying one. Therefore, an investor who is feeling bullish about the stock price will sell the Put.

Once the investor sells the Put, he earns a Premium from the person who buys the Put. This sale means that the investor has sold to another the right to sell the stock at the strike price. If the price of the stock increases and gets higher than the strike price, taking up this strategy will allow the seller to make a profit because the buyer is unable to exercise the Put.

In the event the stock price falls below the strike price, even more, significant than the premium, the Put seller begins to lose money, and the extent to which this loss goes is unlimited.

The Short Put strategy is best used when the investor is feeling very Bullish about the stock price

The risk involved is the difference between the Put Strike Price and the Put Premium (Put Strike Price - Put Premium)

The possible rewards of this strategy are limited to the Premium amount

The breakeven price here is the Strike Price minus the Premium (Strike Price- Premium)

The Long Straddle Strategy

This strategy is also called the Buy Straddle or only, the Straddle. It is a neutral strategy because it takes in the simultaneous purchase of both Calls and Puts over the same underlying stock. The expiration date and the strike price are often the same. It is thought that by having both call and put options, this strategy will achieve huge profits irrespective of the direction the underlying stock price takes. However, this move has to be strong enough.

The best time to take up the long straddle strategy is when the investor perceives that the underlying stock will experience significant tumultuousness or volatility in the days to come

The risk involved is limited to the initial premium

The rewards of this strategy are unlimited

Since there are two kinds of options, the option breaks even at two different points:

The upper breakeven point is the sum of the strike price of the long all added to the net premium paid (Long Call Strike Price + Net Premium).

The lower breakeven point is the strike price of the Long Put less the Net Premium Paid (Long Put Strike Price – Net Premium Paid).

The Short Straddle Strategy

The Short Straddle is the exact opposite of a Long Straddle. This strategy is often adopted when an investor feels that the market will not move much. Therefore, the investor sells the Call or the Put on the same stock, for the same strike price and the same maturity period. This combination results in an income for the investor, and if the market does not move in either direction, the investor gets to keep his Premium. Neither the Put nor the Call is exercised.

The best time to take up the Short Straddle Strategy is when the investor perceives that the investor will see a little volatility in the coming days.

The risk involved in this strategy is limited

The rewards are also limited, but to the premium received

This strategy also has two breakeven points:

The Upper Breakeven Point, which is the sum of the Short Call Strike Price and the Net Premium received (Short Call Strike Price + Net Premium)

The lower breakeven point, which is the Strike Price of the Short Put less the Net Premium, received (Short Put Strike Price − Net Premium).

Calendar Strategies

Calendar strategies, also called time spreads or calendar spreads are suitable for when you are unsure of where the stock is headed. This strategy needs manual monitoring and shut down.

The Long/Short calendar spread in particular, is based on the premise that the premium decays at a faster rate and on dates closer to the expiration date than on those that are further out.

This is a neutral strategy in that it works both for Call and Put options

It is positioned at the sale of a call or purchase of a call, or the shared strike price but away from the expiration date

The risk involved in this strategy is the difference between the front month premium and the back month premium (Back Month Premium −Front Month Premium)

Calculating the breakeven price for this strategy is difficult because of the large number of variables involved

The profit or the returns got from taking up this strategy are limited to the premium of the back month less that of the front month (Back Month Premium −Front Month Premium)

The accounts eligible for the use of this strategy are the Basic margin and other self-directed investment accounts, provided they have prior approval

Taking up this strategy can be tricky because the strategy is dependent on a stock that is not moving, and on proper timing. You are also required to close out the trade manually at the expiration scheduled for the first month.

Buying Straddles

Straddles, otherwise known as a long straddle, is a strategy that works in a neutral market, and it involves buying a put, and a call at the same time of the same underlying stock, price, and the expiration date. This is a strategy that allows for unlimited profit, limited risk options in their strategies, and these are used especially when the trader thinks that the securities under this will experience a lot of volatility in this.

Now, this allows the investor to benefit from a significant move in the stock price, whether it goes up or down, and the approach consists of getting equal amounts of a call and put options with the expiration date. The straddle focuses on a common strike price.

Options are usually a type of security, so the price of this is linked to the price of something else. When you buy options, you get the right, but not the obligation, to sell or buy the asset under it at a set price on or before a date beforehand. A call option gives the investor the right to get stuck and put gives you the right to sell the stock. The stock must rise above for calls or below for puts so that the position is exercised for the profit.

Straddle trade works with a price movement that has a lot of volatility. Let's say there's a company that's working on releasing the latest earnings results in the three-week duration, but you don't know if the news is good or bad. The weeks beforehand would be a good time to add a straddle, since when the report is released, the stock will move sharply higher or lower. So, you want to buy it at a common price.

Let's say that it's trading $15 in April, and then, you have a $15 for the month of June, and it's got a put price of $2, but the price of a $15 call is $1. A straddle is achieved by getting both the call and the put, both of which are 100 and 200 dollars respectively. You'll then have $300 in premium to pay on this. It will increase the straddle if the volume of the stock moves higher, because of the long call, or if the stock goes lower. There is a long call and a long put placed on both of these, and the profits will be realized as long as the price of this moves by at least $3 in each direction. If you know that it's going to be like that, do go for this, but if you don't think the volatility will be more than $3, then this isn't wise for you to do.

You essentially calculate the maximum profit, which is unlimited, and you look at the profit achieved when the price of the underlying is three, and the strike price of the long call and the net premium or price of the underlying, which is lower than the strike price of the long put and the premium paid.

If you get a profit, you're essentially looking at the strike price minus the net premium paid or the strike price of the long put, and the price of the underlying, and the net premium paid on this.

Maximum loss for these long straddles happens when the stock price on the expiration date is trading at the strike price for the options that are bought. At this price, it's essentially totally worthless, and both won't benefit the trader, and the trader will lose the entire initial debit.

There is also the breakeven point, with the upper being the strike price plus the net premium, and the lower is the price of the put, minus the net premium paid.

So, suppose you've got a stock trading at $40 in June, and you decide to have a long straddle there with a Jul40 put and call each for 200 dollars, which is your max profit loss. The biggest amount you'll lose is essentially the option price.

So, if the stock is then trading at $50, it will then make the call in the money, and it has an intrinsic value of $1000 in terms of increase. Essentially, you're pocketing $600 from that trade.

But, let's take it on another level, let's say that you end up seeing them both at $40 at the end of this, and you lose the total profit of what you have. So you're losing $400, which kind of stinks, but it's not the worst.

Essentially, you are possibly going to end up getting a loss and losing only what you paid for the option at most, and you should definitely consider looking at the brokerage commissions as well. It does vary in amount, but they are great for making sure that you have the right volatility strategies in place.

You can also use short straddles, and they are used when you know that little movement is expected at the stock price, again benefitting you.

Buying Strangle

This is the other option when looking to buy based on tends. While straddles don't really have much of a directional basis, the strangle is used when you believe that the stock has a much higher chance of going in a certain direction, but also protect you if you think there will be a negative move.

So, let's say you believe a company will have results that are positive, which means you don't need as much downside protection, instead of buying the put option with the strike price of say $15 for $1, you buy the put maybe at $12.50 with a price of $0.25, which isn't as much. The trade would cost a lot less than the straddle and requires less of a move to break even. The lower strike put option in this protects you against the extreme downside, putting you in a better position and chance to gain from the positive announcement.

It is often called the long strangle, and this one is much more of a neutral strategy than others in trading, and often it does involve sometimes getting an out-of-the-money put, or a call on the same stock and the expiration date being the same too. This allows for unlimited profit again, and limited risk in this, and it's good for options traders that think it will have volatility in the singular direction, rather than both directions. Usually, long strategies are debit spreads, and a net debit is taken in this trade.

This one involves a lot of movement in one way or another direction. For the most part, the max profit is achieved, and you get profit when the price of the underlying and the strike price of the call and the net premium is less than the price of the long put or the net premium paid.

The maximum loss in long strangle is usually when the stock price in expiration is between the strike prices of the options that you get. At that point, both options are worthless, and the options trader loses the initial debit that was taken to enter the trade, so you basically lose the premium. You essentially lose the most based on your premium, and the commissions paid. Usually, the breakeven points are based on the strike price of both of these, and the premium paid, so that's where most of the losses come from.

For example, let's say you've got another stock, also trading at $40 in June. The options trader decides to get a JUL 35 put, and a JUL 45 call for $100 on each of those, so they're $200 in commissions total, which is also the max profit loss. So, let's say that the stock immediately trades at $50 in expiration, which puts the 35 as worthless, but the 45 call is worth it, and since that has a value of $500, you essentially make a $300 profit, since $500 is what you make, minus the premium that you need to pay for all of those, which was $200.

On the flip side, let's say that you notice the company's profit immediately go down to $25, and that gives you a profit margin of $1000, and while the 45 call is worthless, you're going to still get some results from the 35 put, which in turn means that you end up profiting about $800, again because you take the intrinsic value minus the premium.

With these, you need to also take your commissions into account, and while they're small, they're also fees that you will need to pay in order to put that trade in there.

You can also do these short if you want it to spread a little bit when you notice that there won't be much movement in the underlying stock price.

Options strangles are similar to straddles, but this one is good because it saves you as an investor both money and time in trading, especially if you're on a tighter budget.

You may wonder if you should use a long strange or a short strangle. Well, if you are looking to see if there is movement in the longer term, and you think that after a while it will have this change, you can create a "long strangle" position. On the flip side, if you think you're going to only see one quick fluctuation before it's back in the same position it was before, it will then be known as a short strangle. However, no matter what type of strangle you use, the success or failure of this is based on the limitations that you can get, and the supply and demand of it.

There are some factors that affect both strangles and straddles, and here, we'll dive into these three factors to know for both.

The first is the out-of-the-money options. This can be executed using these types of options, and they can be up to half the expense of what the in-the-money options are. It also depends on the capital that you're working with. If a trader puts a long strangle on something, you can trade both at 50% on this, and it can be much less than what the potential loss that you could potentially set yourself up for otherwise.

The other factor is the risk/reward and the limit of volatility. This is a second difference between the straddle and the strangle is that the market might not move at all. The strangle involves the sale of options that may be OTM, and from there, there's a risk of exposure to the risk that there might not be enough change in the asset under this in order to make the market move outside the resistance and support range. For traders that are long in strangles, this might be the worst thing that can happen, but the limited volatility is what can be used to profit from this.

The final factor that plays into positions is delta, which is known as the volatility of this, and it can affect your decisions, in order to show how closely the value of the option changes in ratio to the underlying asset that's there. An OTM option can move up to 30% on some cases, but the best way to determine whether this will benefit you is you should look at the delta of the purchases you're thinking of selling. If you're in a long strangle, you want to make sure that you're getting the maximum move-in option value for what you're paying for. If you're shorting it, you'll want to make sure that this is likely to expire, with low delta, and offset the unlimited risk that should be there as well. Look into each of these and determine for yourself whether or not you're in a position that can be affected by this or not.

If you're dead certain a stock will make a move, you should consider getting a long straddle than a strangle. While a straddle may cost more, the stock won't make such a big move to reach one of the break-even points, so remember that.

Advanced techniques

The following is a list of different strategies that are ideal for exercising options. They include:

Covered Call writing

Collars

Debit and Credit spreads

Naked Puts

Whenever an out-of-the-money is sold, a cash premium is collected. Whatever else happens, you should keep this cash. Otherwise, this trade could end in either of these two outcomes:

The option could become worthless, meaning that the stock price is higher than the strike price, and then the cash collected becomes the returns

It could also happen that on the day of expiration, the strike price is above the strike price. When this happens, the option owner exercises his right to sell the option at the strike price and you will be obligated to buy the shares. This transaction is done spontaneously just as what happens when you are given an exercise notice on the call you sold as you were writing the covered calls.

At the time when you sold the Put option, you were ready and willing to buy the stock at the strike price. However, if you are assigned an exercise notice, you may not want to own the stock any longer. That said, you may want to view the entire situation this way: had you purchased the stock earlier at its market price (at the time you sold the put option), you would have given more money because the price would have been higher. You would also not have been able to collect a cash premium. Therefore, although you are thrilled now, you are extensively better off than if you had bought stock instead of selling the put option. In addition, you can always put the stock back into the market and collect cash

Covered Calls

Covered calls provide one of the best and easiest to use strategies, and beginners can take it up to enhance their knowledge of options. It is assumed that many people dipping their toes in the options market have some investing experience and have traded in the stock market in the past. Therefore, entering the trade through a strategy that supports stock ownership would be the ultimate way to introduce the investors to options and options trading.

For implementation, you need to purchase 100 shares or even more, provided they are in multiples of 100. You could also take up the stocks you own already and sell 100 shares in one call option.

As you sell the call option, some cash premium will be collected, and this amount becomes yours to keep, no matter what comes up in the future. Note that when you write or sell a call option, the following happens:

You may enter into an obligation to sell the 100 shares at a specified price for some limited time, but only when the owner of the option chooses to exercise the option, and you have the exercise notice. The exercise notice is just a message sent by your broker to inform you that your short option has been exercised and that you have sold the 100 shares at the strike price, automatically. This also means that your option position has vanished and that the stock has been taken out of your trading account. The cash from this transaction appears in your account three days after the stock sale has settled. Notice that once you exercise an option, the option ceases to exist.

You lose your say as the seller, and cannot tell whether the option shall be exercised or not. This decision now belongs to the new owner because he has paid cash for the option.

Once you have written a covered call, there are two possible outcomes, and either of them will produce benefits for you:

After the call has been exercised, the stock can be sold at the strike price. You also get to keep the premium given

It could also happen that the option is now worthless after expiration. However, you will beat the game because you will have collected a cash premium. You will still own the stock, and if you want, you could write another call option and get yourself another premium.

Credit Spreads

Instead of venturing into the business of unprotected or naked options, a trader can instead sell Puts, one at a time. The Put purchased becomes an insurance policy, sheltering against loss. It also reduces the potential to make profits, unfortunately. However, the key to success is always to protect against losses while making smaller profits other than opening yourself up to risks that are more significant and enduring heavy losses. Slow but sure increases are better than having your entire investment wiped out. Although optimism in the options market is of benefit, it is more prudent to prevent financial disasters.

Although the credits spread strategy is one of the popular options strategies, and for a good reason, beginners should first understand how to conduct individual options before getting into spread trading. The reason for this is that understanding how a spread works become easier after understanding how an individual option works.

Collars

A collar is one of the most conservative strategies. It is suitable for persons who lean more towards the preservation of capital than towards earning and accumulating a lot of money. The collar takes a bullish position and exposes the investor to limited losses while providing limited returns.

In conclusion, the market is filled with many options trading strategies, but whichever approach you use what should matter in the long run is that you remain systematic and probability-minded regardless of the strategy you take up. This also needs a good knowledge of the market and precision in your statement of the goals and objectives you wish to achieve.

Chapter 3 Risk management and Market

Risk of Option Trading

In trading options, you will invariably encounter risks. For the protection of your investment, it is essential to set personal risk and options parameters within which you will conduct your options trading. These parameters will protect you from the financial shocks associated with trading options. Such parameters include:

The most valuable asset that you must have is knowledge. Having the requisite experience will influence how you will set your settings. You need to understand the types of options available to you and your eligibility for each. In addition, you should seriously consider and fully understand the impacts of losses from those same options. Having this knowledge will allow you to set responsible financial parameters such as you cannot trade in amounts that you cannot afford to lose.

The types of acceptable risks need to some laid down parameters that you need to set out before embarking on trading options. This indicator shows you the level of acceptable risk that you may be willing to undertake. Besides, these parameters limit your exposure level below that which your capital can reliably sustain.

In addition to specific risks, you also need to set out the parameters of dealing with the specified risks and any other associated financial bumps. These parameters will govern how you need to respond and guide you on an appropriate course of action.

Another option parameter is setting the maximum and minimum value estimation of a given stock over a specified period. This parameter allows you to exercise an option when you attain this value. In addition, it discourages unnecessary delays in using options by waiting and hoping for a better deal and a more significant profit margin.

Stop-loss orders will regulate the level of acceptable losses that you can withstand. This mechanism prevents you from running into substantial and significant heavy losses that may lead you into bankruptcy. Having such an order is a protective mechanism as it eliminates emotions from trade while maintaining your liquidity even during off trading periods. You will curtail your emotional tendency to try to break even from a losing trade.

Pitfalls to avoid

You will encounter downturns from time to time, especially during trading. If not dealt with, you may end up burnt out and extremely frustrated. You must know how to handle yourself in these cases to avoid further despair. For making the best out of a bad situation, the following pointers may be of help to you:

Embrace your failure and accept it

Do not avoid addressing your shortcomings, however embarrassing they may be

Take personal responsibility and avoid blaming others

Analyze your actions and identify where you went wrong

Consider whether you would have handled the situation differently

Listen to the opinions and advice of your colleagues

Learn from the situation and rectify your relevant behavioral aspect

Avoid repeating the error or mistake in a similar situation in the future

The Misconceptions and pitfalls of Options Trading

A long call option is useful when you expect a stock price to rise in the future. You engage in long call options whenever you feel very bullish about a particular stock. This strategy is aggressive and relies on your confidence in rising future stock prices. Your potential for profits is unlimited since the expected upward trend maintains trajectory assuming all factors remain the same. However, your risk is limited to the premium since you make losses when the stock price remains or falls below the strike price.

A short call option is strategically opposite to a long call option. In this case, you are hoping and predicting that stock prices will fall in the future. You have to be particularly bearish to engage in short call options. If the stock price follows your predicted downward trend, you make a profit. Short calls are risky since your profit margin is limited to the premium while your risk exposure is unlimited. You may end up with substantial losses should the stock prices reverse direction and start rising in value.

Tips you can apply to succeed in options trading

You need abundant knowledge and experience to trade in options successfully. However, since it will take time for you to gain the relevant experience, you may apply the following tips during trading:

Evaluate your choices

Evaluating your choices before delving into options trading is akin to conducting due diligence. You want to have all pertinent information available to you before investing in options. Such due diligence will put you on a path to eventual profitability in the end.

Failure in conducting this evaluation might lead you to unimaginable losses due to unforeseen pitfalls associated with options trading. Trading in options primarily involves buying and selling of options. You need to have a grasp of all the available options from which to choose. Having a keen eye for profitability will serve you well in the long run. You will soon realize that trading options is quite different from outright buying and selling a stock. You should never confuse these two different investment strategies.

A proper evaluation of available investment strategies will clear this confusion for you. You should first have the knowledge related to options trading and understand all the terminologies involved. You need not just identify the lingo, but learn the meaning of every term in options trading. You will be wise to consult an experienced professional or brokerage firm to get a full understanding of both the advantages and downsides of trading options.

Set your objectives

What do you aim to achieve from trading options? You must clearly state and write down your goal at the beginning of options trading. Your stated purpose should be specific, time-bound, measurable and transparent. Do not set out with abstract goals that do not have any specificity. Such poor objectives include statements like I want to make a lot of money at the end of my options trade.

This goal is not specific enough. A better explanation of objective should sound something like; I will make a profit of X dollars within a Y time frame. Your goal is then specific to the amount of money you will be aiming to make and is time-bound within a specified period. In addition to having a set-out objective, you must develop your investment policy statement. This policy will provide you with strict guidelines to follow during your trading. It protects you from deviating from the laid down course of actions.

In addition, your policy statement needs to identify the potential pitfalls that may hamper your path towards success and provide ways of tackling challenges. You need to promptly devise a way to either avoid or address such challenges according to your policy guidelines. Every investment strategy faces risks and options trading will be no different. You must assess your risks against your objectives and adjust accordingly. Once you have a clear goal, then your decision-making should be focused towards achieving your overall objective by the end of your set expiry period.

Identify profitable options

Your main aim for investing in options is to make profits. Therefore, you need to have an eye or a killer instinct for identifying opportunities that have a high potential for returns. Options trading deal with the potential future stock price movements in a particular direction. You need to be able to predict the next price trend of a given stock correctly based on current factors available to you. It is a test of your speculative ability.

Your ability to identify this trend typically develops with experience. The more you trade-in options, the more your knack to define valuable options will improve. Remember, your options become profitable only if the stock trend follows your earlier prediction. This prediction is also time-bound; hence, your forecast has to come true within a specific period. In direct stock trading, you make profits from increased stock value over time. An options trade makes money from a correct trajectory of the stock price over the same period.

You could predict a downward trend and make a profit if the stock price correspondingly trends downwards over the specified period. However, in a direct stock trade, a downward trend would indicate a loss of value in your particular stock. To increase your chances of identifying profitable options, you need a keen eye for the market trends and any associated factors affecting volatility. Stock volatility is directly related to options profitability. Such a stock guarantees you future price movements, and the only unknown is the kind of trajectory.

Conduct intelligent trades

Now that you have identified your potentially profitable options, it is time to make your entry into the options market. During trading, follow this straightforward rule: You should always make a habit of buying options contracts that are under-priced while selling the overpriced contracts. In addition, you should know when to make your move rather than the number of steps you make. Your timing is more valuable than the quantity.

This way, you end up gaining overall value from your particular option. Historical volatility of a given stock will influence your predictability of the future price movements of that particular stock. Therefore, having available data on this volatility is vital for the profitability potential of your trades. You should not spend a lot of time feeling the market and trying to make your decisions based on your market emotions. When you do this, you will certainly lose your investment. In addition, wasting time in overanalyzing the minor underlying factors affecting stock prices will take too much of your time.

Remember, your options contract is time-bound, and it depreciates, the closer you approach to your expiry date. Intelligent trading is a well-informed piece of business when it comes to trading options. Here are some examples of call and put options that explain the value of smart trading. When you deal in call options, you should buy your option contract at a lower strike price than your projected future value of the associated stock.

When the worth of the stock goes up as you intended the value of your option also rises. Your option contract is in the money and most importantly, is profitable. Once the stock price has gained the maximum amount it possibly can during the period, your best move is to sell your call option. This way, you will have made a significant profit since the only way the stock can move from here onwards is trend downwards.

When you keep waiting for a more extended gain momentum, your option starts losing value since the stock price starts falling. In this case, you either let the option expire and make a loss or exercise its time value and gain some benefit, albeit a small amount. This option roll out would be preferable from your depreciating option.

On the other hand, you own a put option that you are considering to sell. First, you need to buy put options at a much higher strike price than your projected future minimum stock value. Since you expect the stock price to fall over the particular period, your put option remains profitable during this duration. Your intelligent move would be to exercise the option at the minimum stock value.

After the downward trend, the only way the stock can go from here is a trend upwards. When you sell your put option at the stock's minimum value point, then you will have made a significant profit from that trade. However, if you delay exercising your option contract, your contract's value will start falling since the stock price will be trending upwards. Just like the call option, a put option depreciates as you approach its expiry date. In this case, you may avoid a total loss by exercising the option's time value instead of letting it expire.

Mistakes to avoid when Trading Options

You are trading blindly. This practice means that you decide to engage in trading options without a clear objective. Failure to have a set target of what you intend to gain at the end of your trading is risky behavior on your part. You will have no focus, and you will not know when things are not going to plan. You will not have any guiding principles, and you will not know whether your investment is profitable or not. Having a set-out target at the beginning of trading is a way to focus your mind towards achieving a given outcome at the end of the specified period. Your chances of success are higher when you have proper guiding principles towards an objective. You cannot expect to make profits if you do not know how to go about it. Your goal will form a target for you to aim.

Avoid options, which often deal in cash and try to diversify your options. You may encounter shady brokers who insist on dealing with money only. Beware of such personnel and avoid further contact with them. You typically engage in what feels natural to you. Give out your cash in exchange for the right of the option. However, cash options usually end up costing you a lot more in the end. Options have the potential to lose you a more significant amount of money than you invested in starting. You should avoid such contracts due to this unlimited risk potential and the magnified nature of your losses. It is advisable to engage in options assignment where you get stock in return. A stock has an intrinsic value and can generate dividend benefits if properly managed.

Avoid cheap options as much as possible. Your draw towards such options is typically due to the low cost of the contract. You will be tempted to buy these types of arrangements since they are cheap. These contracts are very affordable because they are often not valuable. The agreement will land you out of the money, and you will make losses. You must be wary of the appeal associated with cheap options since you are guaranteed to lose your money. Most valuable options contracts tend to cost a lot more since they have a higher probability of turning out a profit. The opposite argument is valid for cheap options. Remember, cheap is expensive in the end.

You are trading with leverage that you cannot afford. The thrill of making a higher return percentage on your investment may cloud your sensible reasoning. You need to be rational when investing in options. The amount of leverage that you put down has to be an amount that you can afford to lose should the market not go your way. Your mind typically reasons that the more you put in, the more returns you will get. However, you forget the very likely potential for losses. To make it worse, the more you leverage in chasing substantial gains will result in a much more magnified loss. You lose much more than you even invested, to begin.

Trading without an exit strategy. Options trading will not always be all roses and profits. There will come a period when you will spiral from one loss to the next. That is the way markets behave; they are unpredictable. To avoid heavy losses that may end up bankrupting you, you must have a stop-loss order. This condition is a mechanism that will limit your trading in cases where your financial losses become significant enough to affect your financial health. This order gives you a break from trading, which puts a break in your persistent losing streak and saves whatever money you still have left. In addition to stop-loss orders, you could exit the trade altogether. Whenever your option keeps losing money, it is advisable to exercise even if it will be out of the money. Closing out the deal before expiry will gain you some time value rather than letting the option expire worthlessly.

You are applying emotions to trading. This habit is akin to feeling the market. You should eliminate any emotional bearing on your financial decisions. You need a rational mind to make fiscally responsible decisions that have a higher chance of profitability. When you trade under emotional duress, you will be making decisions to please yourself and others rather than meet your objective of making profits. Emotions also lead you to conduct your trades in denial of potential losses. You will end up accruing cumulative losses in an attempt to break even and try to recover your initial investment. You should always remember that emotions cloud judgment and a clouded mind will invariably result in losses.

You are trading with a lack of knowledge and under peer pressure. You should know what type of trade you want to engage in. Furthermore, you should learn all the characteristics associated with your type of business. Your lack of knowledge on an issue or trading just because others are doing it is such a dangerous strategy. You should avoid following the masses because crowds feed on emotions and may lead you astray. To make informed and independent decisions, you should learn your options trading and understand all its difficulties. This way, you will not be caught off guard by a change in stock trend or unexpected losses. Knowing is also a sure way to perfect your skills at options trading, thereby gaining more success.

Chapter 4 Variety of Options Trading

There are different reasons some traders love to use forex instead of the stock market. One of them is the forex leverage.

We will look at the disparities that exist between forex trading and stock trading.

Leverage

When it comes to stock trading, you tend to trade with a cap of leverage of two to one. You must have some requirements on the ground before these can be done. It is not every investor than ends up being approved for that margin account, and this is what a trader needs to be leveraged in a typical stock market.

When it comes to forex trading, the entire system is totally different. Before you can trade using leverage, you need to have opened the forex trading account. That's the only requirement that is out there, nothing else. When you open a forex account, you can easily use the leverage feature.

If you are trading in the United States of America, you will be restricted to a leveraging of 50:1 leveraging. Countries outside of the US are restricted to leverage of about 200:1. It is better when you are outside the US, than in the US.

Liquidity differences

When you decide to trade stocks, you end up purchasing the companies' shares that have a cost from a bit of dollars down to even hundreds of dollars. Usually, the price in the market tends to share with demand and supply.

Paired trades

When you trade with forex, you are facing another world, unseen in the stock market. Though the currency of a country tends to change, there will always be a great supply of currency that you can trade. What this means is that the main currencies in the world tend to be very liquid.

When you are in forex trading, you will see that the currencies are normally quoted in pairs. They are not quoted alone. This means that you should be interested in the country's economic health that you have decided to trade in. The economic health of the country tends to affect the worth of the currency.

The basic considerations change from one forex market to the next. If you decide to purchase the Intel shares, the main aim is to see if the stock's value will improve. You aren't interested in how the prices of other stocks are.

On the other hand, if you have decided to sell or buy forex, you need to analyze the economies of those countries that are involved in the pairs.

You should find out if the country has better jobs, GDP, as well as political prospects.

To do a successful trade in the Forex market, you will be expected to analyze not only one financial entity, but two.

The forex market tends to show higher level of sensitivity in upcoming economic and political scenarios in many countries.

You should note that the U.S. stock market, unlike many other stock markets is not so sensitive to a lot of foreign matters.

Price sensitivity to trade activities

When we look at both markets, we have no choice but to notice that there is varying price sensitivity when it comes to trade activities done.

If a small company that has fewer shares has about ten thousand shares bought from it, it could go a long way to impact the price of the stock. For a big company such as Apple, such n number of shares when bought from it won't affect the stock price.

When you look at forex trades, you will realize that trades of a few hundreds of millions of dollars won't affect the major currency at all. If it affects, it would be minute.

Market accessibility

It is easy to access the currency market, unlike its counterpart, the stock market. Though you may be able to trade stocks every second of the day, five days weekly in the twenty first century, it is not easy.

A lot of retail investors end up trading via a United States brokerage that makes use of a single major trading period every day, which spans from 9:30 AM to 4:00 PM. They go ahead to have a minute trading hour past that time, and this period has price and volatility issues, which end up dissuading a lot of retail traders from making use of such time.

Forex trading is different. One can carry out such trading every second of the day because there are a lot of forex exchanges in the world, and they are constantly trading in one time zone or the other.

Forex Trading Vs Options

A trader may believe the United States Dollar will become better when compared to the Euro, and if the results pan out, the person earns.

The strategy, if it works, can help in affecting the trade when the research pans out.

When you get involved in Options Trading, you tend to get involved in the purchase and sales of options on great amounts of futures, stocks and so on, that will move either up or below at a price during the phase.

It is similar to Forex Trading, since you can easily leverage the buying power to have a controlling power on futures or stocks.

There exist a number of disparities that exist between Options trading and Forex trading. They are:

24 Hour Trading:

When you get involved in Forex instead of Options trading, you have the capability of trading every second of the day, five days weekly. When you look at the Forex market, you will realize that it lives longer than any financial market in the world.

If you have decided to get double digit gains in the market, it is important to possess a generous amount of time every week to carry out these trades. If a large event occurs anywhere in the world, you may end up being amongst the first to benefit from the situation in the Foreign Exchange market.

You don't expect to spend time waiting and hoping that the market opens in the market like in the case of trading options.

With Forex, you can easily trade anytime you want, at all times of the night and day. Whenever you wish, you can trade it.

Rapid Trade Execution:

When you immediately make use of the Forex market; you tend to get instantaneous trade executions. You don't have to be delayed like in the case of Options or some other markets too.

When you place the order, it ends up being filled using the best potential price in the market, instead of wondering what price ends up being ordered.

You won't have to have the urge to slip like the case of options. When you are involved in Foreign Exchange Trading, there is a great chance of liquidity unlike in the case of Options trading.

No Commissions:

Forex market is one that doesn't need commission because it acts as an inter-bank market, where buyers are matched with sellers instantly.

There aren't cases of brokerage fees like in the stock market and other markets.

You will see a spread that exists between ask price and the bid, that is the way a lot of Forex trading firms earn their money.

What this means is that when you trade Forex, you stand to save the brokerage fees unlike in the case of options trading, where you are expected to pay communion since you have no choice but to use a brokerage firm.

Forex Trading Risks

Like every financial market out there, there are risks that one may have to face. The interbank market is known to have different degrees of regulations. Apart from that, forex instruments aren't as standardized as other financial market instruments out there. Do you know that in some parts of the globe, there are no regulations to the forex market?

The interbank market consists of different banks all over the world trading with one another.

The banks have no choice but to determine an asset to credit risk and sovereign risks. They have come up with different internal processes, in a bid to ensure that they remain quite safe. These types of regulations are imposed in the industry to ensure that every participating bank is protected.

The market pricing comes from the forces of demand and supply because the market is made up of different banks giving bids and offers.

The fact that there is a great amount of trade flows in the market means that rogue investors can't influence the worth of a currency. This ensures that there is transparency in the foreign exchange market for those traders that are privy to interbank dealing.

A lot of countries have regulations concerning the forex, but not all do.

Pros and Cons of Forex

First Pro:

When it comes to a daily trading volume in every market out there, the forex is the largest, meaning that it possesses the largest amount of liquidity.

This is one reason that one can easily enter or exit a position whenever he wants, for a small spread in a lot of market conditions.

Cons:

Brokers, banks and dealers are known to give a great level of leverage, meaning that investors can easily control huge positions using a tiny amount of money.

Though you don't see it every time, a high ratio of leverage of 100:1 is possible to see in the foreign exchange market. It is important that a trader knows how to use leverage, as well as the risks that using leverage brings to an account. Using a large amount of leverage has forced a lot of dealers to become bankrupt unexpectedly.

Second Pro

You can trade in the foreign exchange market every second of the day, six days in a week. It usually begins daily in Australia and ends in New York.

The main centers for forex are Singapore, Hong Kong, Sydney, Tokyo, New York, London and Paris.

Second Con

Before you can trade currencies in a profitable manner, you have to understand economic indicators and basics. A currency investor has to possess a great understanding of how a lot of economies function, as well as how connected they are. You need to understand these fundamentals that are able to alter the values of currencies.

Stock Option Trading

What Is A Stock

Stock is sometimes called equity or shares. This is a kind of security that shows proportionate ownership when the firm that issues it is concerned. When a person has stocks, he/she is entitled to a proportion of the earnings and assets of the company.

One can buy stocks and sell them on stock exchanges, but this doesn't mean that there aren't other ways of buying and selling stocks. Stocks can also be exchanged in private sales. There is hardly any investor in the financial world that doesn't have stocks in their portfolio.

Before the transactions can be said to be legitimate, they must be in line with the government regulations that have been put in place to shield investors from fraudulent processes.

When compared to a lot of financial instruments, stocks have overshadowed them.

Stock Vs Bond

Companies give out stocks to raise the needed capital to improve their business or get involved in new projects.

Shares can be gotten in different ways. Sometimes, a person may purchase it directly from the firm when it issues it in the primary market. In other cases, the investor may purchase it in the secondary market from another shareholder. Whenever you see a corporation issuing shares, know that it carries it out because it wants to raise money.

Bonds are in another world of its own. Bondholders are seen as creditors to the firm, and they tend to get interest instead of dividends. They are also paid the principal.

When it comes to stakeholders in a company, creditors have more right over the assets and earnings than shareholders when bankruptcy occurs.

The corporation is expected to pay shareholders first before it pays shareholders during a bankruptcy. Shareholders end up being the last in line and may end up getting nothing or a little amount. What this means is that stocks have higher risks than bonds.

If you can't stomach this, you should avoid going for stocks.

What are The Options

Options are those contracts that allow the bearer to be involved in the purchase or sales of a stipulated amount of asset at a fixed price. The bearer has the choice to buy or not, as long as the contract hasn't expired.

Options are bought like a lot of asset classes by making use of brokerage investment accounts.

Options are strong to the extent that they can improve the portfolio of an individual. They can get this done by leverage and added income protection.

Based on the scenarios at hand, different option situations can suit the goals of an investor.

Let's say a stock market is declining; options can be used as an effective hedge to clamp down on downside losses. One can use options to get recurring income. They can also be utilized for speculative purposes like wagering on where the stock price would go.

The way that free lunch doesn't exist in bonds and stocks is the same way that there is no free lunch with options.

There are some risks that one may face when options trading is concerned. You have to understand these risks before you jump into options trading.

This is one reason that when you have decided to trade options with a brokerage company, you are shown a disclaimer that is similar to this:

Options are members of a bigger league of securities, which are called derivatives. The price of a derivative is linked to the price of another thing. Let's make things more transparent. The derivative of a tomato is ketchup. The derivative of grapes is wine. The derivative of a stock is a stock option.

Options can be said to be derivatives of financial securities, meaning that their worth is dependent on another asset's price.

Some examples of derivatives are puts, calls, forwards, futures, and so on.

Call and Put Options

When we say that options are derivative securities, we mean that their price is related to the pricing of another thing. This means that the other thing is what controls the price of the options.

If you purchase the options contract, you are given the right to buy or sell an asset at a stimulate price before the deal expires. You aren't under compulsion to do this.

When a person has a call option, he is given the right to purchase a stock. On the other hand, when a person is given a put option, he has the right to sell the stock.

You can see the call option as a form of down-payment for something that can be gotten in the future.

Let's use a more explicit example. A person sees a new building going up. He may want to have the right to buy it later but says he won't buy it until it has gotten to some stage, or some other condition has been met, this is an example of an option. He can decide to use the option or not. He isn't under compulsion.

Let's say the developer agrees to give the person the right to purchase the house for about a million dollars at any time within the next three years. Before the developer can agree with this, the prospective buyer has to pay a down payment, which can't be refundable. Within that period of three years, the developer isn't allowed to sell the house to anyone else, until after the term expires.

Chapter 5 Technical analysis

In this chapter, we are going to be talking about technical analysis and fundamental analysis. It is essential that you understand these two concepts, as they will help you tremendously with the growth of your Option trading endeavors. Both of these techniques work very well when it comes to helping you make more profits out of your trading endeavors. Nonetheless, they both have their places. That being said, we will talk about technical analysis and explain to you what it is and the same thing with the fundamental analysis. And then we will help you understand which method works better for what, once you've been able to understand this you will be in a much better position in terms of making more money with options trading.

Technical Indicators and how does they works

To put with technical analysis, it is a way Option Traders finds a framework to study the price movement. The simple theory behind this method is that a person will look at the previous prices and the changes, hence determine the current trading conditions and the potential price movement. The only problem with this method would be that it is philosophical meaning that all technical analysis is that it is reflected in the price. The price reflects the information which is out there, and the price action is all you would need to make a trade. The technical analysis banks on history and the trends, and the Traders will keep an eye on the past, and they will keep an eye on the future as well and based on that they will decide if they want to trade or not. More importantly, the people who are going to be trading using the technical analysis will use history to determine whether they're going to make the trade or not. Essentially the way to check out technical analysis would be to look up the trading price of a particular stock in five years. This is what many Option Traders used to determine the history and the future of the capital, and whether or not they should trade using technical analysis. There are many charts you can look up online to figure out how technical analysis takes place. However, we have given you a brief explanation of what technical analysis is.

When using technical analysis, they also look at the trends that took place in the past. Most of the time, the stock fluctuates simply because of the trends that took place at that time, keeping that in mind, the Traders will look at the future and see if the trends will retake the position. If so, then they will most definitely trade or not trade depending on that's going to benefit them or not. Even though many people would consider technical analysis very "textbook," it is still very subjective. The reason why it is very personal is it because people interpret things differently. Some might think that the past will help the stock, whereas some might think it won't, which is why technical analysis is both textbook and subjective at the same time. The reason why it is textbook is that you have to do a lot of research before you pull the trigger, and it is subjective because the final decision it's going to be based on how you feel about the trade. Many people say that technical analysis as more of a short-term thing; however, some still believe the technical report can be used in the long-term. In our opinion, we think that technical analysis short. The reason why we believe technical analysis is short-term is that we are mainly basing our assumptions based on the past and the trends that took place.

Keeping that in mind, the capital gains you might see from technical analysis might be short-term. Meaning that the tray that you will make will not keep going in the long-term and will be a quick gain for you. Keeping that in mind, technical analysis is a great tool to use for people who are looking to make more money from

Options Trading rather quickly, however, make sure that you do research properly on the stock before you make a trade on it. Many people make a trade on it by looking at the 5-year chart. However, it's much deeper than that you need to make sure that the trends that took place during those five years are going to retake the position. If not, then it will be entirely subjective for you to make a trade or not. The great thing about technical analysis would be that if you do it correctly, you will have a better chance of seeing success from it, and it can build a ton of confidence in new traders. This will be a significant thing for newbies or could be a bad thing for them since you will become extremely confident and make a blunder.

Technical analysis believes that the current price of the underlying asset in question is the only metric that matters when it comes to looking into the current state of things outside of the market, specifically because everything else is already automatically factored in when the current price is set as it is. As such, to accurately use this type of analysis, all you need to know is the current price of the potential trade in question as well as the greater economic climate as a whole.

Those who practice technical analysis are then able to interpret what the price is suggesting about market sentiment in order to make predictions about where the price of a given cryptocurrency is going to go in the future. This is possible due to the fact that pricing movements aren't random. Instead, they follow trends that appear in both the short and the long-term. Determining these trends in advance is key to using technical analysis successfully because all trends are likely to repeat themselves over time, thus the use of historical charts in order to determine likely trends in the future.

When it comes to technical analysis, the what, is always going to be more important than the why. That is, the fact that the price moved in a specific way is far more important to a technical analyst then why it made that particular movement. Supply and demand should always be consulted, but beyond that, there are likely too many variables to make it worthwhile to consider all of them as opposed to their results.

Technical indicators are used in options trading as a way to determine trends as well as potential turning points in the price of underlying stocks. When used correctly, they can accurately predict movement cycles as well as determine when the most profitable time to buy or sell is going to be.

Technical indicators are typically calculated based on the price pattern of a derivative or stock. Relevant data includes closing price, opening price, lows, highs and volume. Indicators typically take the data regarding a stock's price from the past few periods depending on the charts the analyst favors and use it to generate a trend that will show what has been happening with a specific stock as well as what is likely to happen next.

There are two primary types of technical indicators, leading and lagging. Lagging indicators are used to determine if a new trend if forming or if the underlying stock is currently moving within an expected range through the use of existing data. If the lagging indicator points to a strong trend, then there is a better than 50 percent chance the trend will continue moving forward. Unfortunately, they are not especially useful when it comes to determining pullbacks or rally points that may appear in the future.

Alternately, leading indicators tend to come into play when traders need to predict a likely future price point when it is currently unclear if the current price is going to crash or rally. They tend to manifest as momentum indicators which help to determine the strength of the movement of the current trend which will help to determine if the trend is going to continue or reverse. As no trend will continue forever, the momentum indicator will allow you to determine how long of a timeframe your options should be in to ensure that you get out before the disruption begins.

Leading indicators are also useful if you find yourself needing to determine if the price of a specific stock has reached a point where it is unsustainable as this means a slowdown in the price is forthcoming. As overbought or oversold stocks experience a pullback when a slowdown occurs, knowing when this type of movement is coming can thus be supremely useful for several different trading strategies.

Fundamental Analysis

Fundamental analysis is more realistic and feasible in the long term. The whole premise behind the theoretical analysis is that you look at the economy of the country and the trading system that's going on to determine whether it is a good trade or not. More focusing on economics, that's why it helps you to figure out which dollar is going up or down and what is causing it.

One of the greatest things you can do when it comes to Options Trading is to understand why a dollar is dropping or going up. Once you're able to understand that, you will be in a much better position for gaining profits in your Option Trading endeavors. When using the fundamental analysis, you will be looking at the country's employment and unemployment rate also see how the training with different countries overall sing the country's economy before you decide on whether you should try it or not. Many successful Option Traders solely believe in fundamental analysis, as it is factual, unlike technical analysis. Even though technical analysis is accurate, it is not guaranteed like the theoretical analysis. Instead of looking at the trends, you will be looking at what is causing the highs and the lows. Not only that, based on the highs and lows, you will be able to determine the country's current and future economic outlook, whether it is good or not. One rule of thumb to look into with be how good the state is doing, the better the state is doing, the more foreign investors are going to take part in it. Once starting the piece in it, the dollar or the stock in that country will go up tremendously.

The idea behind fundamental analysis is that you need to look at the countries economical, and you also need to look at. To make you understand, what fundamental analysis is it is mostly when you invest in a country is doing good in the economy, and not invest in a company when they're doing wrong in the marketplace. Which makes sense since the economy dictates how high are low prices going to be per dollar? Most of the time, investors will invest the money as soon as they see the dollar going up. The reason why they will do that is that they know the dollar will keep climbing up since the economy is getting better. One of the great examples would be when the US dollar dropped in 2007 2008, and the Canadian dollar took up, at that point, a lot of investors are investing in Canadian dollars of the US dollar. After a very long time, the US dollar was dropping tremendously, whereas the Canadian dollar was more expensive than the US dollar. This was one of the anomalies which took place back in the day. If you were to use technical analysis in this instance, then you will not get a lot of success out of this economy drop. Which is why fundamental analysis could work a lot better or most people in the long-term and in the short-term, which is why many top traders recommend you follow fundamental analysis instead of technical analysis to find out which dollar you're going to be investing in?

Leading Indicators and How does they works

Now we get into the part where we show you which method to use and when ideally when your Options Trading, you would like to dabble with technical analysis and fundamental analysis to see optimal success. However, you can do fundamental analysis and see progress, both long-term and short-term. In our opinion the best way to go about it would be to try out technical analysis in the short-term, the reason why we think the technical analysis, in short, would work very good for you is that it is something that you can't go wrong with if you do it properly. As we explained to you what technical analysis is, you can see why it is so good for someone to start with technical analysis and to see amazing results out of it. Another thing technical analysis can help you out with would be that it will help you to build up your confidence in the beginning. When you're starting Option Trading, especially in the beginning, you must build up trust, and you make yourself believe that you can, make money from Options Trading.

This will help you to continue with your Options Trading journey and to learn more; more accurately help you to start investing your money the right way and to continue off becoming a full-time Option Trader. Once you have dabbled with technical analysis, you can start doing your more long-term trades with fundamental analysis. The only problem with fundamental analysis would be that there's a lot more research to be done, and if you're trying to make Options Trading a long-term income Source or a full-time income Source, then the chances are you should be doing your research before you make a trade. Keep in mind that, fundamental analysis will help you to keep going in the long-term and will yield you the best results possible. Even though technical analysis has a higher success rate, fundamental analysis will be a lot more long-term. Secondly, the more you do fundamental analysis, the easier it's going to get for you.

Keeping that in mind, the best method to go about Options Trading, in the beginning, would be to start with technical analysis make small trades, and make some money. This will help you to build up your confidence with Options Trading and therefore help you to keep going on. The second thing you should be doing is research on the fundamental analysis I'm slowly started dabbling with it until you are sure on which dollar or stock on investing based on your research. You will require some brainpower to dabble with Options Trading using fundamental analysis. However, once you understand it and start dabbling with it, you will see the success they looking for with Options Trading. The final verdict would be to use both of them however used technical analysis, in the beginning, to really see some short-term benefits out of it and then eventually branch off to fundamental analysis and then dabbing our professional analysis trading there to see the small incremental games. When combined, both you will be in a much better position to make a lot of money from Options Trading.

Indicators are an important part of any trading activity. They do exactly what their name implies, they indicate. They can indicate when to get in or out of a trade, or what the market players are gravitating towards – buying or selling. They can also tell us if a stock or ETF (exchange-traded fund) is in an oversold or overbought condition, or if the market has resistance or support at particular price points.

They do tell us a lot, don't they? If you know how to use them. Let's discuss how we can use indicators to help us make decisions when buying and selling options in particular. There are many indicators, but to keep things simple for beginning option traders, let's consider just a few of my favorite and reliable indicators for trading options.

First, two categories are included in most trading charts. They are listed in different places, an indicator tab or a drawing tools tab. Let's discuss the ones located in the indicators section and then the drawing tools section.

Indicators

Bollinger Bands

CCI – Commodity Channel Index

Stochastics

Bollinger Bands – Named after John Bollinger, who created the indicator with a certain set of parameters to help identify trends. Bollinger's bands can also help you to visually see potential areas of support and resistance along with historical volatility.

How it works - Bollinger bands have an upper and lower boundary with a middle boundary that is a moving average. The idea is that normal prices will stay within a 2-standard deviation from the normal 95% of the time. John set the bands to encompass 95% of the security's price movement and based the 2-standard deviations on a 20-day moving average, so when setting your parameters on your charting system, you want to use a 20-day period with 2-standard deviations, as John intended for their use. Many platforms will have a default of the 14-day period.

How to use - Visually, you will see the bands constrict and go sideways during consolidation and expand or widen during breakouts or high volatility. When the bands constrict, volatility is low in comparison when the bands are wide apart. Pricing, represented by candles on a chart, can only sustain a candle's close above the Bollinger band no more than, usually, two candles (on any time frame used) before they must fall back within the Bollinger framework.

Since option traders are very watchful of volatility, this visual can quickly help you to identify when volatility is high or low for entry and exit points. Option traders exit during periods of high volatility and enter ideally during periods of low volatility.

Just because the bands have widened doesn't mean we immediately sell our options contract; we may miss out on the biggest part of the move.

However, when we see the candles closing above the bands one or two times, and it's nearing our expected target, we can confidently decide to sell our option knowing we can capture the best price at the highest point of volatility. This takes the mystery out of when to sell, Great, huh!

When the bands constrict and start to go sideways during times of consolidation, volatility is low, and this is the point option traders want to consider buying a call or put (or both) waiting for a breakout in one expected direction or another and enters the period of high volatility.

I must add, while Bollinger bands are a great indicator, using it alone is not recommended. Use it with other indicators such as CCI or a Stochastic indicator to confirm what you are seeing.

We purchased a short-term contract on Oilu when the Bollinger bands were constricting during low volatility. The ITM put option contract price we paid was $240 per 100 shares. Two days later, the price quickly moved down with high volatility, and we see the two candle closes outside the Bollinger bands. We could choose to get out at this price point if we were using the Bollinger bands as our sole indicator, and we still would have made a tidy profit of $170 when we sold the option contract with a limit sell order of $4.10.

If we add a support line (we'll discuss those later) for pricing, we could stay in a little longer to see if it hits the support before bouncing back higher, and would have sold the option contract at $4.70 for a tidier profit of $230 per contract. Nice!

I hope you are starting to see the value of using indicators to help you make a good decision. You can use indicators to help you with entries and exits and getting better buy pricing during times of low volatility and better sell pricing during times of high volatility. Bollinger bands are my favorite tool with options, but I still use two other indicators fit for options trading in conjunction with Bollinger bands that help to confirm my opinions. When all three are in agreement, things work like clockwork. Let's discuss those two others now.

CCI/ Commodity Channel Index – This indicator was originally developed to use with commodity trading, but I found it works with stock too if you alter the settings a smidge. It really is considered an oscillator that works by swinging from one extreme of the scale to their opposite extreme in an exaggerated response to price movements. It follows the candles located in the chart above it and moves with the candle movements in a magnified manner; this magnification causes it to swing from one side to the other (top to bottom) which indicates oversold and overbought conditions. I use this oscillator on a 1-hour chart only, it is not really good for lower time frames, although sometimes you can see it as a good pattern on lower time frames on some stocks, but not for all.

Overbought is an extreme price condition where buyers consider the prices too high; this condition is not sustainable because eventually, the buyers stop buying deeming it too high.

Oversold is and extreme price condition as well, only the prices are considered too low and ripe for buying.

The CCI indicator is a visual barometer of how much of an overbought or oversold condition exists in a stock or ETF.

How it works – The CCI indicator consists of 3 vertical lines with a wavy line running through all three from top to bottom.

 The top line is measured at 100 and signifies an overbought condition

 The middle line is neutral or zeroes which are usually consolidation points

The bottom line is measured at -100 and signifies an oversold condition

The measurements that we are using are the 200 and -200 overbought and oversold extremes.

How to use – First, adjust the settings within the indicator for the default periods from 20 to 30 which gets rid of the choppiness in the price movement, and makes it easier to read and identify the extremes within the 200 and -200 ranges.

This indicator also moves in conjunction with candlesticks and measures the difference between a security's price change and its average price change. The CCI is a leading indicator that tells us when a drop or a surge is in play from overbought or oversold conditions.

A drop below or above 200/-200 tells us there may be an undercurrent of change coming soon, but we are going to wait until it continues to cross under or above the 100/-100 line before we take any action (100/-100 are still oversold conditions, just not extreme). If the Bollinger bands and stochastics agree we can start looking at option contracts for puts and calls. We would buy a call if it reaches the -200 line and then continues to cross the -100-line moving up. We would buy a put if it reaches the 200 line and continues down and also crosses the 100-line moving down.

I've never traded this ETF before finding it on FinViz as a search example for this book, but when I added all my indicators to the chart and saw how everything was aligning for a good put position. I was able to make a quick, confident decision to buy a put, knowing that past experience said this would work out to a good profit. The more you use your system, the better you are at spotting good opportunities.

Stochastic– is a simple oscillator and adds a third opinion to our charts. It is a moment indicator developed in the 1950s by George Lane and measures momentum by comparing the closing price with the previous trading range over a specified period of time. It shows the most recent closing relative to the previous high-low range.

How it works - In simpler terms, it follows and measures the speed and momentum of the price. The stochastic indicator is also a leading indicator because the indicator changes direction before the price itself does.

The most known use for this indicator is bullish and bearish reversals when the indicator has diverged from the price, which anticipates an upcoming price reversal. You can see this on your charts when the stochastic lines are moving up, and the candles on the chart are moving down or vice versa.

As I said, it's a simple indicator with just two lines top and bottom and two wavy lines running between the top and bottom.

How to use – Learning to identify reversals in price takes more practice, but I'm confident you can learn it over time. For option purposes, it is a good confirmation for overbought and oversold conditions, confirming a change in price direction.

If you use more than one indicator and they all align, this gives you more confidence that your opinion is correct, and you can take the appropriate action.

Topline set at 70 for overbought conditions

Bottom line set at 30 for oversold conditions

When the two lines hit the bottom 30 line, and the two wavy lines cross each heading up this means prices are heading up after an oversold condition, for how long is unknown. This is a good time to close a put position when it nears your target.

When the two lines hit the to 70 line, and the two lines cross each other heading down after an overbought condition, prices are heading down. This is a good time to close a call position when it nears your target.

Support and Resistance Lines

Support and resistance are where prices in the past had a challenge penetrating. When you draw (using your drawing tools on your charting platform) support lines are the bottom of the candles and resistance is the top of the candles. There can be many areas of support and resistance, but some areas are more supportive or more resistant, otherwise known as major resistance/support areas. These are areas in the past where consolidation appeared. Breaking resistance means it will most likely travel to the next area of resistance or support.

When we added the support line to our chart we were able to see that prices may have a little further to drop, even though our two price candles closed below the Bollinger band giving us an opportunity to close our put option position, we chose to wait for a better price when prices hit the support level.

By having this knowledge, we were able to still get out of the option contract quickly, but obtain a better price by waiting a little longer for prices to hit our target at a major support level.

Drawing Trendlines, Support and Resistance Lines

Practice drawing support and resistance lines on your charts using the drawing tools most platforms provide. It's easy, zoom out on the chart so you can see it over many months, then draw a line connecting all the peaks, is it sloping up or down? Sloping up is a current uptrend, sloping down is a current downtrend.

You have just drawn trendlines, now that you have the trend in your visual site, draw a horizontal line across all the peaks, these are the support and resistance areas. When you see a lot of candles across the same line area, this is the major support or resistance. When trending up, these are your resistance areas, and when trending down, these same levels become your support areas. Get the picture?

Trendlines are drawn between two peak points, the more that line up the better. You can have one peak that penetrates the trendline if you have three connecting peaks or more in the same trendline and still have a valid trendline.

When the price candles fall below the trendline in a meaningful way, a change in trend is underway. We always want to follow the trend in options trading. However, different time frames, like a daily chart, will give you a view of the long-term trend and 1-hour to 15-minute charts will give you a view of the short-term trends. When multiple time frames agree in trend direction you have a more stable trend, but if you are trading a short-term options contract on shorter-term charts, be aware, the longer-term trend can reassert control over the direction, unexpectedly.

Now that we have our trendlines in place, it is time to draw our horizontal support and resistance lines.

Again, use your horizontal drawing tool supplied by your charting platform and place a line on the top of each peak. These are your areas of support and resistance.

POE'S (Points of Entry/Exit)

We've already discussed how placing market orders can be a detriment on your fill price. Part of options trading is getting good prices for your option purchases, so it doesn't eat into your profits. We already pay brokers' commissions on both sides of the buy and close, so the last thing we want to contend with is cutting down our profit expectations because of bad fill prices.

There is another way you can avoid a market order, and still enter an option at the best possible price, at the time you place it, without having to readjust your limit order up each time the market price is above your desired price. This strategy is the "walk limit order." Let's cover how to do this in more detail.

No one likes to chase the market's price, you'll never come out ahead, but constantly changing your limit order feels like you ARE chasing the markets, and it's a chore to go into your account and go through the process of changing your well thought out order.

The "walk limit order" tells your broker to go in and change it as many times as it takes to get filled, up to a certain price that you are still willing to pay.

Here's how this order works. You set the parameters to start at a certain price and how much to walk it up after a predetermined time increment. You also pick the price you want to begin at and your final price. If it hasn't filled by the specified time to buy, say an hour, then it turns into a permanent GTC limit order.

If this routine can save you .06 cents on a purchase of 5 contracts that would save you in total $30, and if you were able to accomplish this savings by using walk limit orders 3-5 times a month, you'd be saving $90-$150 on your option purchases per month. Here's a screenshot of what a limit order screen might look like, depending on your platform.

In this example we see the "walk limit order" under order type, this is for a vertical call debit spread, and if it is not filled within the day, it will drop off or cancel since timing is not GTC but a day order. The start price to fill is .25 cents ($25) and increases by .01 cent ($1) increment every 2 seconds until price reaches the final price of .34 cents ($34), at which time it would remain as a day order until the end of the day and cancel.

Now you have two efficient ways to fill your options orders without taking a bath on price and without using a market order.

Getting into a trade is usually easier than getting out, and so it is a good idea to make an effort to plan your exit strategy in advance. There are three exit strategies you can make use of to exit and close an option contract at the best possible price or the very least a good price.

I've already discussed limit orders as a way to enter a trade at a good price, and the same is true for exiting at the price you want. This is a great way to exit when you know how much your option should be worth for every $1 the underlying stock goes up. Remember, Delta tells us how much the premium increases with ever $1 the underlying stock price moves. Don't forget to add Gamma, which tells you how much the Delta number increases with every $1 move of the underlying stock. If you recall, Gamma helps you be more accurate in your price prediction. When you use a limit order, you can enter the price in advance right after your fill, if you have the numbers, then wait for the move in your direction and your order to be filled. That's the beauty of knowing how to use Delta and Gamma!

If you don't want to mess with Deltas and Gammas, you can use this next strategy as long as you accurately know your target price of the underlying stock. It's called the contingent order.

Contingent Orders

Don't beat yourself up too much if Deltas and Gammas irritate you; many traders use contingent orders because they have specific situations they trade under and know when they want to be out of a position, but don't always know what the option will be worth at the point they want to close their position.

Here's how it works – If ABC stock moves above $59.11 in price, and you want to get out, this type of order will only trigger when ABC trades above $59.11, at that point it opens as a market order, if it gets filled before market close the position is closed, if not it stays as a GTC order and when the market opens it will be filled since it is a market order.

Here is when/how to use it – If you know your target price, you can enter your desired price target (do your research - know what specific target you want, not a guess) as a contingent or a conditional order.

If you broker makes this type of order available to you here are the contingent criteria that need to be filled out:

Choose the contingent or conditional order tab

Enter QuantityPrice = Market

Duration = Day

(You want to be filled if it hits the price today only, if not use GTC for whenever it hits that price, last for 90 days).

Trigger = Price

Symbol

Choose Last Greater$Price you want it to trade above

Market on Close Order

This is rarely used, but it's useful if you simply want to sell your option at the close of the trading day. There are some unpleasant aspects of this type of order, and you only want to use it as a last resort. You need to make sure it is on liquid options. Otherwise, you may get filled horrifically because the bid/ask spread on some options will cause you to get a fill you weren't counting on.

If you are on vacation in a remote location, and your option was expiring while you were there and given you hadn't closed it before you left, this might be a good option for you, but other than that, I can't think of a time I would want to expose my profits to this type of order.

I only mention it, so you know your choices no matter what type of situation you end up in.

Let Your Options Expire?

Sometimes people are afraid to let their options expire, but there are some instances where it is better to let them expire or even exercise your options as an exit strategy. For example, if the commissions only add to your loss don't incur the selling expense, let the options expire.

If you want to hold the stock in your portfolio, and the strike price is a reasonable one, you could exercise your option and hold the stock until it went in your direction, then sell all or some to cover the losses you may have had by selling them at a loss. Of course, this is if your portfolio can cover the amount needed to purchase the shares.

Chapter 6 Best Options Secret Strategies

Are you ready enough to face the world of trading and other business options? Do you think you already have the skills and knowledge needed to make your trading business work?

Making your trading business work will not only depend on your resources, knowledge, or skill. There are still lots of aspects that need to be given enough attention and focus. This is when options secret strategies will come your way. With these, all your aspirations and ideas to later imply on your trading business will be all possible and results effectively. Given this, here are the strategies needed to be applied to your trading business to make it more capable of reaching success.

Long Call Options Trading Strategy

Starting with the first one – the Long Call Options Trading Strategy refers to the strategy that can provide an opportunity for your trading business and its processes to create huge profits when the stocks are increasing with even a little amount of money at risk. This is best, especially when compared to the cost or amount of buying shares of stock. Long call options trading strategies do profit from higher levels of stock prices, so the main goal of using these kinds of strategies is to choose the stocks you believe and think that will arise in price soon.

Call Option Function

A contract of call option provides the option buyer with the right to buy or purchase the underlying stock at its specific price. This is what we call as the strike price. An option also refers to the time-limited contract that has an expiration date by which it must be sold, exercised to buy stock, or allow to get expired.

A lot of varying trading options is in stock against it with expiration dates that are ranging from half a dozen. Also, there are varying strike prices below or above the current price of the stock. Buying calls on a certain stock is the meaning of having a long call option. Short positions in options are given to the seller of the calls.

Long Call Strategy

Buying the call options on a particular stock may let you think that about an increase in the basic long call strategy. One example is: per share, the stock is at the price of $50, and you always think that it can increase up to $60 or even higher. You can buy call options with $50 as the strike price and $3 for the cost.

When the stock increases above $53, the long call option trade can be profitable, and when the earnings up to $100 for each dollar, the stock can increase above the $53.

The stock of 100 shares is for each option contract, so an option with $3 can cost you $300 and $1 as the share price gain is $100.) Using the option value will help in increasing the stock price, so you can easily and effectively sell the options to lock the profit in.

Long Call Spread

Another strategy included in the long call options is the long call spread. Adaptation of this strategy allows you to gain profit from a small price gain coming from the underlying stock. The call spread mainly deals with the purchasing of call options in one strike price and offers calls at a higher price strike. For example, on a stock that costs $50, you can buy the $50 worth of strike call for only $3 and offer or sell the $55 worth of strike call for only $1. Given this, your net cost can be $200. With this kind of strategy in trading, you can reach satisfying results, as well as the profit position whenever the stock reaches or overcomes the $52 per share.

Also, a call spread can limit your maximum profit in between with the minus for the strike prices and the cost of every spread. For this example, you can enable yourself to make a total of $300 for every spread when the stock had reached $55 or even higher.

Consider Potential Losses

For the last but not the least strategy is what we call as consider potential losses. Not all the time, we are just going to live a happy life without any hardship or problem. There is also a time when problems and hardships are present. Life is not all about rainbows and unicorns, take note of that. However, what if for every loose a better and effective trading strategy, as well as an opportunity comes along?

This is the time when considering potential losses mustn't be treated as a ghost but rather an opportunity. Losing trading does not mean being a fool and not skilled at all. It is only a representation of the things that need to be fixed and repaired once malfunctioned.

The more you lose in a trading process, make it sure to establish the trading strategy needed for its further development and success either through doing a spread or purchasing phone calls. When the price of the stock already reached low to its bottom line or finally got expired, a total of 100% loss will be given. When the stock increases above the strike price, intrinsic value is gained by the long options that can be taken through selling and offering the options.

For example is when the stock approaches the expiration date with $51 as the cost, you can sell and offer a $50 strike call option for the cost of at least $1 that can let you earn $100.

Short Call Options Strategy

Do you think it is already enough? But wait, there's more!

Another set of strategies that can be used in dealing with trading processes and methods is the Short Call Options Strategy.

Overview

This strategy mainly encompasses the bearish to neutral options of trading strategy that aims to capitalize on premium decay, moving in vitality downwards and moving in the underlying asset downwards. But it isn't only a neutral or bearish strategy. In the underlying asset with slightly positive movements, selling calls can also work.

Because of the risky nature of getting involved with the short call, almost all of the options brokers are requiring to have special approval to do trading with this strategy. It is because of the theoretical undefined, or unlimited, and potential loss.

Key Points:

Selling the call options comes with a theoretically undefined risk.

Short calls can't be covered unlike of selling the put options.

When the stock price stays what it is, increases, decreases, or move slightly, short calls can be a profitable one.

Selling of call options in the cheapest and the best online broker can be done in the Ally Invest.

$0.50 for every option contract will be charged.

In 2018, out of the lots of online brokers that work 24 hours per day service, the Ally Invest topped for its lowest commission in trading the short call options strategy, as well as the free and best options trading software.

Defining Short Call Option Strategy

Note: Just like the other option strategies, selling calls in-the-money or ITM, at-the-money or ATM, or out-the-money or OTM is possible. Unlike any other short put, selling the short calls will never be covered until the seller owns an underlying asset in an appropriate amount. A covered call is the name of the underlying asset strategy that is owned. When the trader sells and offers a put, there will always be a defined loss for the trading processes. It is theoretically unlimited for the naked short call as its maximum loss. Given this, the short calls are defined as naked or uncovered options positions.

Short Call Option Strategy Example

If the stock ABC is trading at a share of $50, 52 calls can be sold for the cost of $.30.

Maximum Profit and Loss

Maximum Profit= Premium Received

Maximum Loss= Unlimited

Summary of Short Call

Maximum Profit is defined.

Maximum loss is undefined

The risk level is very high

It is best for stock price collapses, does not make any move, or slight movements only.

Trading can be done when you want to short a stock and to collect the premium.

Legs= 1 leg

Sell call is the construction.

The long call is the opposite position.

Break-even for a Short Call

For a short call, the breakeven point is equal to the premium received and the strike price of the short call.

In the example mentioned above, the point of breakeven at the expiration for selling 1 call in stock ABC will be $52.30. Also, the stock ABC can increase up to $52.30 for every share at the expiration before the trade start to lose money. Because of this is referred to as a break-even point at the expiration, ABC can trade with $52.30 mainly to the expiration, and short calls of $52 will be at a loss because of the $52 call premium time built into it.

Why Trade Short Calls?

Great question, isn't it?

You may be afraid in the first place to trade short calls, but here are some points that can enlighten your understanding. Trying out new things and strategies for your trading business can make it possible for it to achieve its goals and dreams. Also, there is nothing wrong with taking risks for it can only make your trade a lot better and mature to face other upcoming problems. For now, let us answer the question.

A large pool of traders can go and deal with the entire careers in trading without even selling a single call due to its high level of risk. There are also lots of options that traders keep on looking exclusively to sell premium, and short calls are what they make as their go-to strategy. Why?

This is mainly because of almost all the parts, an upside and smaller fear with the short call option strategy than the presence of the selling puts. When selling covered or naked puts, there will always be a risk that can make the underlying asset to crash and go back to being zero. If this kind of situation happened in your trading options, then it would truly be destructible for the position of the shot put.

For 99% of the upside tail-risk, capable of being option assets, can simply be different from the downside tail-risk. The possibility may be slim that a particular asset can cash and go down, is priced usually into puts, and this is the main reason why to put tend to trade much wealthier than the calls.

Basically, mitigation of risks of a widespread crash of the market that can wipe out the underlying asset can only happen when you sell calls.

Risks behind the Short Call Option strategy

The only exception of this downside vs. upside theory of risk is with the individual stocks and commodities. Selling of calls using commodities brings a unique set of possibilities than the indices of stocks, for example. On the rare occasion, specific kinds of commodities including wheat, soybeans, corn, and others, have crashed already up to 20% because of the events encompassing the forecast such as the droughts and changes in weather. These kinds of natural phenomena can be the cause of the extreme shortage of supply and send a skyrocketing increase in the prices of the commodities.

If you have 10 lots of short calls on features that are wheat-based, it can be a nightmare when the wheat had opened up in the next coming day having 25%. This is the time when the call premium sellers are at risk or in trouble.

Moreover, by having the individual stocks, especially the so-called beta stocks, it is entirely conceivable to gap up to 40% for a stock on the news from the upgrade of an analyst, increased dividend, buyout offer, and a lot more.

Due to the possibility like this one, a large pool of traders is looking forward to selling call options on indices that are capable of being an option such as SPY, RUT, NDX, and SPX. The massive index chances, just like the S&P 500 trading, increases up to 25% the whole night is unlikely. Given this, it sorts of eliminates short call composed upside tail-risk, though not the entirety of it.

Short Call Margin Requirements

To employ the strategy of a short call option, the required amount of power will depend on the exchange rules, level of account approval, and the requirement of the broker. As the general rule in every typical account of margin, 20% of the underlying asset is being required for every naked or uncovered call.

Also, the requirements for short calls can depend on the underlying asset. The volatile stocks can have an increased amount of requirements. The future short call options work under the US SPAN margin, and it is equivalent to the individual stock's portfolio margin.

The very best way for you to determine the impact of the margin on selling calls is to preview it before the transmission process into a live account.

What is Theta or Time Decay?

Another vital aspect when dealing with the short call options strategy is Theta. It is also referred to as the Time Decay. It is a favorable matter for the short calls that are ATM or OTM. Theta depends on the number of days still available before it reaches the expiration date. However, the time premium is priced out of the calls. Also, the collection of premium drives the traders much more effectively to sell the calls. When the expiration date had finally come, theta will decay, and it is a certainty. The rest of the components can inflate in its prices.

Call Selling Tips to Consider

Option premium will only be gained through effective and worthwhile selling of calls. With OTM-type short calls, money can be generated if the stock increases, declines dramatically, or just does nothing. Even though three ways are technically helping to generate money through short calls, it is vital to always keep in mind that call selling is a bearish trading strategy option at heart.

Sharp development and increase in price and vitality of the underlying asset can destroy havoc on the position of the short call. Given this, sharp decreases in price and vitality of the underlying asset and being added to the theta decay can make the process of call selling highly profitable. This is due to the volatility- being the major component of the price of an option.

Call selling must be done without having any means as the sole strategy of a trader but an unequivocally and incredible strategy to sell option premium effectively. All of those can be done and achieve without having any market crash risk or financial crisis.

Long Put Options Trading Strategy

Another set of strategies that can be used when dealing with trade and other related processes is the Long Put Options Strategy. This kind of strategy is referred to as a basic strategy in trading options wherein investors purchase put options with the standing belief of the underlying asset's price is significant under the striking price before the upcoming expiration date.

Short Selling vs. Put Buying

In comparison with the stock short selling, it is much more convenient to bet off the stock through the purchasing of put options as you don't need to borrow stock can short. Also, the risk is being capped with the paid premium for the put options. It is as opposing to the risks that are unlimited when underlying stocks are short selling.

But there is a limited lifespan for put options. When the price of the underlying stock does not make any move under the strike price beforehand its expiration date, it will expire being worthless.

Limited Risks

The risks upon the implementation of the long-put strategy are very limited depending on the paid the price for every put option regardless of the amount of stock price is referred to as trading on the expiration date.

Here is the formula for the calculation of maximum loss.

Maximum Loss= Paid Premium + Paid Commissions

Maximum Loss in times of Underlying Price >= Long Put's Strike Price

Points of Breakeven

The price being underlying at which the break-even is reached for a long put position is capable of being calculated through the following formula.

Breakeven Point= Long Put Strike Price- Paid Premium

Short Put Options Trading Strategy

Selling of put options can obligate you to purchase stocks at the strike price A when there is an assigned option.

When selling the puts without having any intention of purchasing the stock, you are aiming for the puts to be sold and to expire being worthless. This kind of strategy has only a low potential profit compared to the previous ones. The stock had remained above the strike A at the expiration, however potential substantial risks when the stock eventually decreases or goes down. The reason why most of the traders across the world are running this kind of strategy is that there is an increased possibility of achieving success when selling OTM puts. If it happens the market steps against you and your trading, you must have a plan in place called the stop-loss. As this strategy unfolds, it is recommended for you to watch and observe it properly. This way, you can enable yourself to generate effective remedies or solutions to any kind of interruption that might come in hand.

Chapter 7 3 Actions for Intermediate Traders to Get Their Feet Wet

1. Writing covered calls

This is a strategy that is considered much safer than outright purchase of stocks. It is generally referred to as CCW or covered call writing. It should be among the initial strategies to initiate as an intermediary trader. There are reasons why this approach makes sense.

1. The strategy is easy to understand:

With this strategy, you will simply sell your rights to purchase stocks at a specified strike price to another trader. After collecting the payment from this sale, you await the lifetime of the agreement to expire as it is limited. Should the buyer decline the opportunity to purchase the stock after the deadline, then your obligation to sell the shares will no longer exist.

2. Covered call writing provides plenty of beneficial trades compared with stocks purchase:

Basically, if you the value of your stock declines, you will only lose out less than the trader who did not have a covered call. You will earn a profit when the stock price drops lower than the cost of the premium you collected.

Should the stock price remain largely unchanged even upon expiration dates, then you will earn a profit while other investors such as those who buy stocks will only break even. You also earn more should the price of the underlying stock rises beyond the strike price at prices lower than the collected premium.

This profit is also greater than direct stock investors. Should the related stocks experience a massive price increase, then this is the only situation where your earnings will be less compared to those of a buy and hold investor.

3. Covered call writing or CCW offers some protection, albeit limited, against any losses should the markets decline

Basically, when you collect money from the sale of the call option, you will have reduced the financial liability on the underlying stock.

What is a covered call?

We can define a covered call as basically an options trading strategy where you enter a long position in an underlying stock and then sell or write a call option based on the same stock. This is a strategy designed to generate multiple streams of income.

As an investor or trader, this is a strategy that you will use when you have a short-term neutral opinion on a particular stock. In such cases, an investor would hold onto this position for a while holding a short position while still earning an income. The term "buy-write" is another name used to refer to covered calls.

Covered calls – set up

The covered call strategy is considered a neutral strategy because traders mostly expect minimal rise or fall in the price of the underlying stock price for the entire life of the call option.

Basically, covered calls are not ideal for bullish traders or investors. Bullish traders should hold onto the stock rather than write a call option. The option will essentially cap the profit, and this will negatively affect the overall profit should the stock price go up.

Covered calls basically operate as a short-term hedge on a long position. This way, an investor or basically a trader gets to earn a profit from the profit received after selling the call. The challenge is that the investor will lose any gains the stock makes on the market. Also, if the call buyer decides to exercise their right to buy the shares, you will have to forfeit them.

This option strategy is also not suitable for investors who are very bearish. Such investors and traders should consider selling their stocks on the open market. This is because the premium received from selling the call option may not sustain any losses incurred by a losing stock.

Best profit and loss scenarios

With a covered call option, the maximum profit that you can get is equal to the difference between the strike price of the short call option and the buying price of the underlying stock added to the premium obtained. The maximum loss will occur when the premium received is larger than the cost of the underlying asset.

How to write a covered call

First, select your preferred stock within your portfolio of shares. Identify the stocks that you could be open to selling and avoid those that you consider very bullish especially in the long term. This way, you will not feel disappointed should you lose a stock which would otherwise have become profitable in the future.

Next, you should identify the strike price that you are comfortable with. This is the price at which you are happy selling the stock. The best approach to identifying the right strike price is to pick one that is out-of-the-money. The reason for this approach is because our aim is for the stock price to increase before it has to be sold.

After this, you need to choose the appropriate expiration date for the call option contract. The most ideal in this case would be one that is 30 to 45 days in the future. However, this is only a guide, so consider the dates carefully. The best date is actually that which allows you a good premium if you sell the option at the chosen strike price.

2. Buying LEAP Calls as a stock substitute

Another great way of making money as an intermediate options trader is investing in long term calls, also known as LEAPS. The aim of buying long-term calls is to enjoy benefits that are the same as those of owning the stock. However, buying the call option would limit your risk and exposure. In such a situation, the LEAP call would act as a substitute for your stock.

What are LEAPS?

We can define LEAPS as options that you buy for the long-term. They are considered a long-term investment that acts as a substitute to actually owning shares. In essence, you get to benefit from LEAPS as you would if owning the underlying shares.

The acronym LEAPS stand for Long-term Equity Anticipation Securities. Generally, any stock options that have expiration dates more than 9 months are considered LEAPS. Such options are similar to other options with the only difference being that they have a longer "life expectancy" compared to ordinary options.

The LEAP set up

Basically, if your thoughts on a given stock are bullish, then you can consider using LEAPS arrangement. This way, a simple rise of about 50 points could translate to a rise of over 300% which is highly profitable. Even then, there are risks involved, so it is crucial to be wary. Basically, use caution and apply this strategy wisely. If you do so, then you will be able to leverage your investment greatly.

In most cases, LEAP stocks often have an expiration date beyond one year while sometimes it is at least 9 months.

This strategy allows you to invest a relatively small amount of money and buy options rather than spend larger amounts buying actual shares. Using this approach and strategy, you will be able to earn huge returns especially if you make the correct decision regarding the movement of the shares.

How to get started

The first step in investing in LEAPS is identifying the appropriate stock for this strategy. Simply follow the standard procedure of purchasing a stock at the stock market. To determine the most ideal stock for this strategy, you will need to do some research. There are websites where you can get useful information that will help with the analysis. Take for instance Ally Invest Quotes + Research. Do some fundamental analysis of the stocks until you find one that gives you enough confidence.

Once you determine the most suitable stock for this strategy, you will need to determine the strike price. Basically, you will need to invest in a stock option that is deep in-the-money. This basically means a stock whose strike price is lower than the stock's current price. If you apply this strategy, then aim for a delta that is equivalent to or higher than 0.80 based on your chosen strike price.

This delta reference simply means that should the stock price go up by $1 your chosen stock option should rise by at least $.80. The same reasoning applies if you choose a stock whose delta is 0.95 which means that for a stock price increase of $1.0 then your stock option price will rise to $0.95. This is basically theoretic. Anytime you use the Options Chains on Ally Invest; you will be able to see the deltas for each listed stock.

The starting point

When you want to invest in a LEAPS strategy, you should consider one in which the in-the-money stock price is 20% or higher. For instance, should the price of the underlying stock equal $100, then you should choose a call option whose strike price is lower or equal to $80 but not more. But if the stocks are volatile, then you should consider that it is even deeper in-the-money in order to acquire the kind of delta that you need. However, you should note that your option becomes costly should you go even deeper in-the-money. The reason is that the option gains a lot of intrinsic value even though the upside is a higher delta value. When your options have a higher delta, the better they will serve as a stock substitute.

Expiration date

Always keep in mind that all options have an expiration date, include long-term options. Always keep this in mind. Now, should the stock price ascend sharply after the expiration date, this will do you no good at all. Also, as this date approaches, most options tend to lose their value at a pretty fast rate. Therefore, you need to be extremely careful with these dates.

When it comes to this particular strategy of LEAPS, then you should always opt for options that have at least a year to expiration. This is advisable as you will have sufficient time to benefit from stock movements in the course of the year without the burden or expense of actually buying the stock. Remember that in the end, this strategy is adapted for investment purposes where you want to make large sums of cash rather than just a speculative tool.

Precautions when using LEAPS

One of the biggest precautions or risks when using this strategy is to use it as a risky gambling tool rather than the investment vehicle it was meant to be. For instance, some traders may select stock options with bad pricing or those that may probably never strike.

At other times it may be the case of piling risk upon risk by choosing long-term, less costly stocks for this strategy. Such options may not even fit the definition so LEAPS because the expiration period may be less than 9 months. Sometimes traders make speculative trades and put themselves at high risk.

This strategy may not be suitable for all investors so please approach it with care and understanding the inherent risks involved. Pursue this strategy when you have the cash to spare and stocks that are just right. However, if you adopt the measures indicated and follow the right procedures, then you should be able to benefit immensely from this strategy.

3. Selling cash secured puts on stocks you want to buy

This is a put option that is secured by cash. The strategy involves simultaneously drafting a put option while putting money aside for the purchase of the underlying stock should they be assigned. The end goal of this strategy and every other is to generate a lucrative income or a big enough profit.

Defining a cash-secured put option strategy

The cash secured strategy is where an investor or trader sells a put option in order to acquire a stock or other security that they need to buy but at a significantly lower price than the actual cost of the security.

The strategy includes writing an out-of-the-money or at-the-money put options while at the same time securing money to purchase the underlying stock should the need arise. The main aim here is to actually acquire the targeted shares at a much lower price compared to the prevailing market prices.

This way, you will acquire upfront the option premium and in return the obligation to buy stocks at a lower price. If the situation was ideal, your stock would trade at a price that is above the strike price of the option for the life of the option.

Take the ideal situation where your stocks trade at levels higher than the option's strike price for the lifespan of the option. Should this be the case, then you will not have to purchase the underlying stock but still receive payment for the option premium. However, this is only one scenario out of a possible three distinct scenarios.

Apart from the ideal situation described above, it is possible that the stock price will fall to low levels that are below the difference between the option premium and the strike price. In such a situation, the trader or investor still fares well the adjusted cost basis is more attractive compared to what is available on the open market once the premium received from the option is accounted for.

The remaining scenario occurs when the stock price falls to levels that are well lower than the strike price less the option premium. Under such circumstances, an investor's adjusted cost basis fares much worse than direct access via the open market. This is even after the option premium received earlier is accounted for.

Determining the secured puts to sell

There are a couple of characteristics that you need to be on the lookout for. For instance, identify stock options that have between 45 and 60 days before expiration. Also, look out for strike prices with approximately 1 standard deviation below the prevailing price at the markets.

Basically, you need to also keep in mind the fact that cash-secured puts enable traders to create a passive income stream from money that is lying idle in your bank account hoping to invest in blue-chip companies at a much lower price compared to the prevailing market rates.

The strategy

In this instance, you will be selling your put options with the hope of acquiring the underlying asset. While still pursuing this strategy, you probably should consider selling in the open market your out-of-the-money put. By doing this, you are of the opinion or hope that the stock will fall below the strike price and maintain that level. This is essentially a bearish move. As such you will be assigned the stocks that you were hoping to receive, and they will belong to you.

Tips and advice

The first rule of thumb when trading the cash secured options put is to never go overboard with any of the leverage available to you especially when trying to sell put options. As it is, if you are like most traders who purchase 100 shares per single trade, then you should work with a single contract that equals 100 shares. Should you prefer selling or buying 200 shares then make it 2 c0ntracts of 100 shares each.

Therefore, first, sell the put option at the preferred strike price. Make sure that as you implement this strategy, you will be required to set aside some money in the form of cash. This money will then be used to purchase the underlying stock should you be awarded. Also, the stock price is most likely to be higher than the strike price you determined earlier.

This strategy is appropriate for traders with at least some basic experience as well as all other advanced traders. Investors at all levels are able to execute cash-secured puts. It is an ideal strategy to apply if you are bullish in the long term and bearish in the short term. At expiration time you will only break even if the strike price is less, the premium received cancels out.

You will suffer the maximum potential loss when the stock price drops to zero. Your losses in this instance will be limited to the strike price. Basically, the potential loss can also alter to the long stock position should the puts be assigned as well. You need to make sure that there is sufficient cash amount available in order to take care of the costs of purchasing the shares should need to purchase the stock arise.

Under this strategy, time decay is actually favorable. It is advantageous when the option price sold bends towards zero level. This will imply that it will be less costly to buy the option back when you choose to close a position before it expires. You will also benefit if there is IV or implied volatility.

Once the strategy has properly been established, you will benefit if the implied volatility decreases. This is because IV will lower the price of the stock option that you just sold to other traders. This will make it less expensive for you when the position is closed prior to expiration. Since there is collateral within this specific strategy, it is highly recommended that you ensure that you have experience trading options before actually attempting this trade.

Chapter 8 Daily Routine for a Trader

Missteps occur in options trading. They regularly happen on the grounds that an excessive amount of data is coming in without a moment's delay and you feel overburden, froze, and forceful, or they frequently happen during calm/bring times when your watchman is down. Furthermore, obviously, there are constantly irregular mix-ups, for example, hitting an inappropriate catch – purchase rather than sell – or putting out an inappropriate position size. Such blunders can even occur with robotized methodologies.

Before each trading day take a couple of minutes to experience multi day trading routine to help limit mistakes for the duration of the day. Here are the means to experience. Contingent upon the market you exchange, you may wish to include a couple of extra advances. This entire procedure just takes a few minutes however spares you a great deal of dissatisfaction and cash.

1 Conditions in the Market

Make a brisk appraisal of trading conditions up until now. Is the pre-advertise demonstrating a great deal of instability, or is it steady? Is there a pattern or explicit propensities you take note?

Such an evaluation tells you how to continue, and whether you ought to exchange your framework by any stretch of the imagination. This is particularly significant if utilizing an emotional framework – a framework that fluctuates marginally dependent on economic situations. For instance, in unpredictable conditions, you may have a bigger expected benefit focus than on multi day when there is no unpredictability.

2 Keep Notes

On your graph, put content notes expressing when high effect news discharges are. Whenever fascinated in an exchange you may disregard one of these occasions, and it could cost you beyond all doubt. Record it on your diagram. In the event that the occasion happens later in the day, look over and put the content note close to the estimated time of the declaration. That way you will see it when the opportunity arrives.

3 Launch Platform is Vital

Dispatch your stage. Ensure statements are gushing (not slacking or sporadic) and the program is running easily. Most intermediaries give dependable information encourages, yet issues can emerge. In the event that the information feed is irregular or appears to be erroneous, don't exchange until the issue is fixed. On the off chance that it looks right, continue.

4 Automated Strategies Should be Confirmed

Regardless of whether you day exchange physically, you may have some robotized orders. For instance, in Ninja Trader and Meta Trader, you can convey stop misfortune requests and focuses on the minute you enter a position. Ensure these stop misfortune requests and targets are set properly. In the event that trading with a "robot," ensure all settings are exact before beginning it.

5 Have an End Time

In the event that you see a time you pattern to give back benefits all the time, compose a note to yourself to quit trading around then. Numerous informal investors will in general lose cash in the time encompassing (and including) the New York lunch hour, if trading U.S. markets. In the event that you see this inclination, don't battle it. Quit trading during portions of the day you commonly lose cash. Help yourself to remember this when you start trading every day.

6 Have a Starting Position Size

In the event that you exchange with a default position size, ensure it is set fittingly. Adding an additional digit to a position size could spell catastrophe. Dropping a digit implies you exchange a small amount of what you could have, and you pass up a chance.

On the off chance that you physically change your position size dependent on your entrance point and stop misfortune areas, note your record balance before trading. Legitimate position measuring limits risk to a little level of record capital, for example, 2%. In the event that you have a $40,000 account, you can risk up to $400 on an exchange. Remember this greatest risk for the duration of the day (or compose a content note on your screen) to remind yourself this is the most you can risk on one exchange.

7 The Economic Calendar Must be Considered

High effect monetary occasions can cause value spikes/holes, making critical slippage (the distinction between the value you expect and the value you get) on stop misfortune orders. It's ideal to abstain from being in exchanges for the couple of minutes encompassing high effect planned news occasion. Check your monetary schedule before trading, and note the high effect news times. For U.S. stocks and prospects, you can utilize Bloomberg. For Forex, look at the Daily FX financial schedule.

On the off chance that you exchange individual stocks all the time, check the organization does not have income or different declarations due out that day. The Yahoo! Finance profit schedule functions admirably. Know about these occasions, to abstain from trading directly before the declaration.

8 Important Thoughts

Help yourself to remember your risky propensities, and how you will deal with those circumstances should they emerge. Go over your Key Trading Thoughts.

9 Be Mindful as You Start Trading

You are set to exchange. This procedure should help dispense with certain errors identified with position size, trading an inappropriate record/contract, trading during news or just not setting up your brain to exchange.

As you begin searching for potential exchange arrangements, remember your Key Trading Thoughts. This will help keep you out of awful exchanges (ones not in your trading plan) and keep you caution and prepared to jump on great chances.

10 Use the Right Trading Account

In Meta Trader and Ninja Trader (for instance) you can sign in to various records utilizing a similar stage. Ensure you are trading the right record. Be particularly cautious on the off chance that you practice day trading in a mimicked record, yet additionally have live records. You would prefer not to have an incredible day, just to acknowledge you traded in recreation rather than with genuine capital. In the event that day trading prospects, ensure you are trading the right most noteworthy volume contract. Know about termination dates on the agreements you exchange.

11 Make a Trading Routine

Your day trading routine may shift marginally from this, contingent upon your trading style and the market you exchange. Make a daily schedule however. It just takes about a moment or two to experience, and can spare you from a great deal of dissatisfaction.

Conclusion

Thank you for taking the time to read this book and finish it all the way to the end! I hope that you have found it to be informative and educational. Options are an exciting way to get into trading, and the potential is there to make quick profits! To any beginner, things may be a bit too complex with all the jargon that is involved, however, take the time to learn and understand what each concept means and soon things will be much easier. Also, you are here for one purpose, to know how to trade with options and earn profits!

Hopefully, you will take the lessons at heart to mitigate your risks and trade carefully. The first principle to follow in this regard is only to put as much money as you can afford to lose into the stock market. That way, in the event of total loss, you would still be able to go ahead and carry on with your life, and possibly raise more money later to try again.

Of course, with options, it is not necessary to get into a situation where you "lose your shirt," because you can start trading options by only spending a few hundred dollars. This means you can take small risks and build up your account slowly. There are going to be some losses, even the best traders experience losses. But, if you proceed carefully, you will learn how to trade effectively, and you can rack up more wins than losses.

The best thing to do in order to get started is to buy some calls and puts on index funds. Start small, let your account grow and accept that you are going to have some losses along the way. That is the reality when you decide to work with this type of investment or business – there is a risk for losses along the way. But that does not mean that losses will be a constant thing. If you play your cards right, really study the market and make sound decisions – you are bound to rebound from your losses and start gaining profits. Risk is in everything that we do, and it all just varies depending on how we mitigate these risks and make them work to our advantage. We cannot predict how the market will fare daily, stock prices are affected by a lot of factors, and most of them are things we cannot control, that is one of the things that you need to keep in mind.

www.ingramcontent.com/pod-product-compliance
Lightning Source LLC
Chambersburg PA
CBHW070638220526
45466CB00001B/221